A
SURGEON IN KHAKI

Through France and Flanders in World War I

By

ARTHUR ANDERSON MARTIN

Introduction to the Bison Books edition by

GLYN HARPER

UNIVERSITY OF NEBRASKA PRESS

LINCOLN AND LONDON

Manufactured in the United States of America
∞
First Nebraska paperback printing: 2011

Library of Congress Cataloging-in-Publication Data
Martin, Arthur Anderson, 1876–1916.
A surgeon in khaki: through France and Flanders in World War I /
Arthur Anderson Martin; introduction by Glyn Harper
p. cm.
Originally published: New York: Longmans, Green & Co.;
London: E. Arnold, 1915.
Includes bibliographical references.
ISBN 978-0-8032-3492-5 (pbk.: alk. paper)
1. Martin, Arthur Anderson, 1876–1916. 2. World War, 1914–1918—Medical care. 3. World War, 1914–1918—Campaigns—France. 4. World War, 1914–1918—Campaigns—Belgium.
5. World War, 1914–1918—Personal narratives, New Zealand.
6. Surgeons—New Zealand—Biography.
I. Harper, Glyn, 1958– II. Title.
D630.M27A3 2011
940.4'752—dc22 2010044191

INTRODUCTION

GLYN HARPER

When Dr. Arthur Anderson Martin left New Zealand in April 1914 for a short tour of surgical clinics in the United States, Britain, and Europe, he had no idea that the international order was about to change nor that he would soon be caught up in major world events. These immense changes and his long journey afforded Martin a unique opportunity to become an eyewitness to some of the key battles of the First World War. Unfortunately, it would eventually lead to his death on the Somme in September 1916.

In 1914 Dr. Martin was the senior surgeon at Palmerston North Hospital. Despite the small-town status of Palmerston North—some ninety miles north of the capital city of Wellington, where he had resided for the last eight years—Martin's qualifications, experience, surgical skill, and pioneering attitude won him a reputation usually only accorded to specialists in much larger city hospitals. One of his medical interests was the treatment and surgery of cancer patients, and by 1911 Martin had established in Palmerston North the only radium institute in the North Island for this purpose.[1] One of the objectives of Martin's short tour in 1914 had been to obtain further clinical information and financial support for this venture.

The first hint that Martin's plans were to be interrupted occurred in Aberdeen at the annual general meeting of the British Medical Association, where Martin was the New Zealand delegate. As he recorded in *A Surgeon in Khaki*, most of the delegates knew something was amiss when their German counterparts were suddenly withdrawn, having been ordered to take an urgent passage home. The British declaration of war soon followed.

The day after this declaration, Martin traveled to London to offer his medical services to the British War Office. There was little likelihood that a surgeon of Martin's experience would be turned away, especially as he had previous experience of war surgery. Martin had been a civil surgeon with the South African Field Force, and his surgical cases from field hospitals in Natal and The Transvaal featured in *British Medical Journal* articles and had been the subject of his MD thesis (which he completed in 1903).[2] Little wonder that with all this experience the thirty-eight-year-old Martin was disappointed and somewhat offended to be given the rank of temporary lieutenant. As he stated with some bitterness: "Seniority or special skill or previous war experience mattered nothing." There was little Martin could do about his lowly military status but make the best of it and soldier on.

One of the strengths of *A Surgeon in Khaki* is that it fully illustrates the chaos, confusion, and lack of preparedness for war of the British Expeditionary Force (BEF) in 1914. Only by skillful negotiating and some serious horse trading was Martin able to obtain a full military uniform. Even then he never did obtain the revolver and sword that medical officers were expected to carry and that Martin was told were absolutely necessary for him to function effectively as a military surgeon. As Martin astutely noted though, several pairs of rubber gloves for dressings and operations would have been much more useful. There is also a certain timeless quality to *A Surgeon in Khaki*. The "hurry up and wait" that all soldiers will know, the confusing and often contradictory orders, the "spy mania" of 1914, and the wild rumors of enemy advances and retreats all feature in Martin's book.

Also featured are Martin's eyewitness accounts of the great events of 1914. Martin arrived in France in time to witness the battles of the Marne and the Aisne and traveled to Belgium, where he observed the First Battle of Ypres. While Martin disliked Belgium intensely, finding it "dirty and uninviting" and the Flemish "sullen, dour and suspicious," he rightly predicted that Ypres would soon become a place of pilgrimage given the intensity of the fighting there. Martin recorded with a surgeon's objectivity the German atrocities that occurred in France and Belgium, which he described as "nauseous and disgusting frightfulness." Too often these atrocities have been ignored or dismissed by many historians as British propaganda. Martin described the hatred that soon developed for German snipers, who, while operating in accordance with the rule of war, were somehow regarded as unsporting—"not cricket" to use Martin's term for it. Martin also recorded several executions of German spies, the terrible effects of artillery on both sides, the effects of aerial bombing, and scenes of destruction and devastation. This keen observer then asked of this "ghastly horror": "Where could one find here a trace of the glory, pomp and magnificence of war?" It was not to be found in this conflict, and *A Surgeon in Khaki* is a remarkable account of the war's destructive power, even in its earliest months.

Another key strength of this book is that it reveals how unprepared and how out of touch the Royal Army Medical Corps (RAMC) was in 1914. Hints of this occur early in *A Surgeon in Khaki* when news arrives of the retreat from Mons and Le Cateau. More than fifteen thousand casualties were awaiting treatment as a result of these military reverses, but Martin recorded with brutal honesty "that the medical arrangements had quite broken down." At this stage of the war, though, Martin still maintained "a sublime faith" that somehow the British Expeditionary Force, including the RAMC, would muddle through this crisis. In the coming months Martin's "sublime faith" would be sorely tested, and he would be instrumental in forcing through changes to some of the RAMC's more outdated practices.

One test occurred because of the lack of motor transport available to the RAMC. For years motorized ambulances had existed, and Martin regarded them as the best means of transport for a wounded or sick man. As he recorded with a degree of incredulity: "Yet in spite of the lessons of army manoeuvres in this country, and of the dictates of reason, our Army Medical Department sent Field Ambulances to the front with the old horse-ambulance of the days of Napoleon and Wellington, and did not have a solitary motor ambulance where they were so vitally necessary."

To resolve this "odd and incomprehensible" situation, Martin wrote to several people in positions of authority back in the United Kingdom stressing that urgent action was needed. One of his letters eventually reached Lord Kitchener, the Secretary of State for War, and motor ambulances soon started appearing in France. While Martin's actions produced results, they could hardly have endeared him to his RAMC superiors. However, as Martin acknowledged, if motor ambulances had been available when the BEF landed in France: "Many lives would have been saved, and much suffering . . . avoided." That, above all, was what mattered to him.

Martin was shocked by the lack of equipment being carried by RAMC Field Ambulances in 1914. He believed that a Field Ambulance should carry all the necessary equipment for emergency surgery—including for the treatment of serious head and abdominal wounds. But in 1914, the Field Ambulances were regarded as first-aid stations only and lacked the vital equipment for surgery. In fact, surgery was avoided as much as possible, and when performed it was of a "crude and temporary nature." Martin found this situation intolerable, believing that the equipment carried by the Field Ambulances "leaves very much to be desired, the whole organisation will be thoroughly reorganised and remodelled, and that there will be evolved a medical unit more in consonance with the modern conceptions of good clean surgery." But in 1914 many of the basic requirements of good clean surgery were lacking. Martin had to send to London for a supply of needles and catgut and in the meantime was forced to use silk thread on septic wounds, which he admitted was a "very bad surgical technique." Performing a dangerous operation on a knee joint, Martin could not get sterilized towels, gloves, an aneurism needle, or a pair of scissors—basic surgical tools. As Martin confessed: "It made one despair. Yet, all of these things should have been at hand, and could have been easily obtained by the exercise of some forethought." These were serious criticisms.

There was one "new and totally unexpected complication" of wounds that Martin recorded without criticism. This was the onset of gas gangrene, which became "one of the terrors of the doctors at this time." Caused by a group of bacilli prevalent in the soils of France and Belgium, gangrene cases caught the RAMC by surprise, and at first its doctors did not know how to prevent or treat it. If a wound became infected, it usually meant an amputation was necessary to save the life of the patient. This "heartrending" discovery was outlined by Martin.

In *A Surgeon in Khaki* Martin also advocated what was to become his modus operandi as a battlefield surgeon. He believed that the first treatment received by a seriously wounded soldier was critical to his chances of survival. A skilled surgeon, surrounded by the necessary equipment and in a sterile environment, should perform the necessary surgery as soon as possible, Martin believed, even if this placed the surgeon at some risk. Martin's advocacy and practice of immediate specialist surgery as near to the action as possible was featured in the *British Medical Journal* and was widely acclaimed. Such surgery, often under artillery and small-arms fire, was also incredibly risky. Martin's practice of this immediate surgery saw him mentioned in dispatches by General Sir John French in 1915 and by General Sir Douglas Haig in 1916. It would, however, eventually lead to his death.

In early 1915, after eight months of service in the field, Arthur Martin was released by the RAMC to return to New Zealand. His RAMC superiors were probably glad to have such a critical and influential member leave their service. Between the time of his leaving the RAMC and his arrival in New Zealand Martin wrote most of his account of his experiences, which was to become the book *A Surgeon in Khaki*, published in 1916. The book was an immediate success and came to be regarded as a classic account of frontline medical conditions and battlefield surgery in the early months of the First World War. It remains an important historical source for developments in military medicine in particular and also for the history of the first few months of the First World War in general.

Immediately after arriving in New Zealand, Martin was appointed to a commission investigating the outbreak of measles, pneumonia, and cerebrospinal meningitis at the country's main military camp. These outbreaks at Trentham Camp, just north of Wellington, had been serious, and over thirty soldiers had died as a result. Martin was appointed as a medical member to the commission, as some leading politicians thought that his reputation would add some medical weight to the commission's findings.[3] Following his service on the commission, Martin returned briefly to Palmerston North but soon became active in training the Field

Ambulance of the newly raised Rifle Brigade. What became the 3rd Field Ambulance was then based in Awapuni, a suburb of Palmerston North, and it was only to be expected that a surgeon with Martin's experience would be involved with its training. However, when the 3rd Field Ambulance left for France, Martin sailed with it holding the rank of senior major in the New Zealand Army Medical Corps.

The New Zealand Division's first major action on the Western Front occurred on 15 September 1916 when it took part in the third phase of the battle of the Somme. This day, 15 September, was also significant in that the tank made its first appearance. Several had been allocated to support the New Zealanders, although most suffered mechanical failure before and during the battle. The Rifle Brigade was in the thick of the action from 15 September, and two days later Arthur Anderson Martin was mortally wounded near the village of Flers while treating wounded soldiers in the front line. He had been hit by shrapnel in the abdomen, face, and neck just after 3:00 p.m. and died in the Amiens Base Hospital later that evening.

The history of the New Zealand Medical Service records: "His book 'A Surgeon in Khaki,' published in 1916, made him known and admired by a wide circle of readers, but to his friends his breezy nature, his attractive personality, and his strong confident optimism, made him very dear, while in the field he was bold, resolute, resourceful and brave to a fault. He was not to be spared; we could ill afford to lose him."[4]

In fact, the New Zealand Rifle Brigade suffered five medical officer casualties on that day, with another gifted surgeon, Captain Gilbert Bogle, being killed in action. So severe had been the loss of medical officers in the New Zealand Division that the senior medical officer issued special instructions warning his doctors to avoid unnecessary risk and not to proceed beyond their advanced dressing stations except under special circumstances.[5] This was a much more cautious approach than Martin had advocated and practiced.

The death of one of the country's most gifted surgeons was mourned in most of New Zealand's newspapers. The news came as a great shock to the people of Palmerston North, as its local newspaper recorded:

> The news of the death of Dr. A.A. Martin came as a great blow to the people of Palmerston, amongst whom he was held in reverent esteem both for his skill as a surgeon, his sterling character as a man, his worth as a citizen, and his proved courage and devotion as a patriot. The announcement of the sad occurrence, which arrived by cable early in the evening, was followed by a perfect deluge of enquiries on the telephone at this office, and

> confirmation of the sad news was followed by the keenest expressions of remorse and eloquent testimony of the esteem in which the deceased was universally held.[6]

New Zealand had indeed lost one of its finest citizens. On 1 January 1917, Martin was posthumously appointed to the Distinguished Service Order.

A Surgeon in Khaki by Arthur Anderson Martin is an important book and one that deserves revisiting. It records an eyewitness account of some of the most significant events of the First World War. It records the dire state of the RAMC in 1914 when that service was struggling to cope with the demands of total war in an industrial age. It outlines important changes in battlefield surgery techniques, changes often forced upon the medical authorities by the harsh realities of war and the overwhelming number of casualties being inflicted. Above all, it records the skill, dedication, initiative, talent, and courage of military surgeons like Arthur Anderson Martin. As the history of the New Zealand Medical Service acknowledged, these were men the belligerent nations could ill-afford to lose, and yet in the First World War these men had to be placed at risk and many became casualties as a result.

But then the First World War, that great destroyer of people, places, and families, did not care about merit, talent, and skill. It did not discriminate between ordinary soldiers and gifted military surgeons like Arthur Anderson Martin. It took them all.

Lest we forget.

NOTES

1. Brian Mather, "Martin, Arthur Anderson 1876–1916," *Dictionary of New Zealand Biography*, http://www.dnzb.govt.nz [updated 22 June 2007].

2. Mather.

3. Mather.

4. Lieutenant Colonel A. D. Carbery, *The New Zealand Medical Service in the Great War 1914–1918* (Auckland, 1924), 212.

5. Carbery, 212.

6. Obituary, *Manawatu Daily Times*, 21 September 1916.

PREFACE.

In the following pages an attempt is made to record, however imperfectly, some of the scenes, and the impressions formed, during those great days of 1914 when our army was fighting so stubbornly and against such odds in France and Flanders.

The notes in many instances are disconnected, but the things seen presented themselves in a disconnected way, and if they are not all beautifully dovetailed one into another, they are at least given forth somewhat in the way in which I viewed and received them myself.

During the actual progress of this war, and when the war is happily over, much literature bearing on the great struggle will be produced, but I venture to think that of the personal narrative and the personal impression one cannot have too much.

The narrative includes my experiences at Le Havre, Harfleur, and the battle of the Marne, the march to the Aisne, the wait on the Aisne, the move across France to the new lines behind La Bassée, and the final move to Flanders not far from Ypres.

ARTHUR A. MARTIN.

CONTENTS

b

LIST OF ILLUSTRATIONS

École Jules Ferry at Bethune
Trenches in Flanders
Monsignor distributing medals to Belgian soldiers at the roadside
Going towards the trenches at Ypres
French soldiers going to the trenches

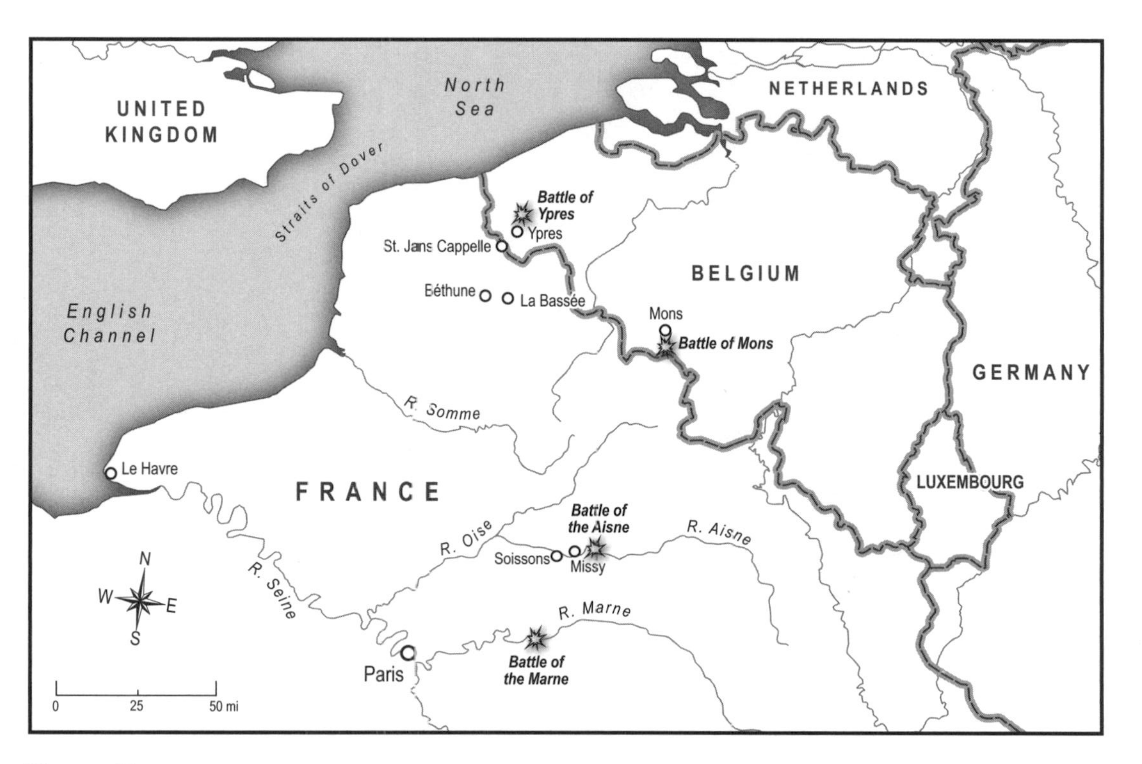

WESTERN FRONT, 1914

A SURGEON IN KHAKI.

CHAPTER I.

FROM PEACE TO WAR.

EARLY 1914.

IN April 1914 I left my practice in New Zealand for a short tour through the American, British, and Continental surgical clinics.

After having visited all the important clinics in the United States—the famous Mayos of Rochester, Murphy's at Chicago, Cushing's at Boston, and others at Cleveland, Baltimore, and Philadelphia, I finally arrived at New York.

When visiting the clinic at the German hospital at Philadelphia, I, with other visiting surgeons, principally Americans or German-Americans, was invited to tea and cake, or cake and beer, in the reception-room of the hospital.

As the day was very hot we all drank iced German lager beer, and, when leaving the room, were presented with a gilt " wish-bones " holding ribbons of the German national colours.

All of the American and German-American doctors

wore the ribbons on their coats, but I put mine in my pocket as a curio. I did not wish to be thought to have German sympathies, although I had drunk their lager beer. In New Zealand the Germans have never been appreciated as they have been in England. Perhaps the air of the Pacific gives one a truer perspective of some things as they are.

At New York I delayed sailing two days, in order to avoid a German boat, and reached England by the Holland-American boat *Rotterdam* in July. We had on board the *Rotterdam* a very large number of Germans, and as usual they were chiefly noticeable for their great prowess at meals, and for their noisy method of eating. They drank much "good German beer" and filled the rooms with German smoke and German gutturals. They are not attractive fellow-travellers.

On arriving in England I proceeded to Aberdeen, where the annual meeting of the British Medical Association was being held, and to which I was a delegate.

At Aberdeen we had a very large number of foreign representative surgeons and physicians and men from nearly every part of the world. As usual there were many Germans and a few Austrians.

We were struck by a very curious incident towards the end of the meeting—last day of July. The president of the Association, Sir Alexander Ogston, gave a reception to all the delegates from the British kindred and affiliated associations, and to the foreign representatives. Although the German and Austrian delegates had been about in the morning, not one was present at the evening reception. They had all departed silently, and had said good-bye to no one.

Germany and Austria had sent out their messages, and the medicals returned with all speed.

We were then on the eve of war, but none of us at Aberdeen thought that we would be in it, or that we were then rushing swiftly to great events.

The Austrian note to Serbia was being discussed. Germany's action was doubtful. Russia plainly said that she would not stand by and tamely see Serbian Slavs humiliated by their powerful neighbours. In spite of the cloudiness of the political atmosphere and the slight oppressiveness none really expected lightning and thunder, or that any spirit would

> In these confines with a monarch's voice
> Cry Havoc! and let slip the dogs of war.

On the 3rd August Sir Edward Grey, in the House of Commons, in a serious speech, reviewed the European situation. With convincing eloquence he showed how anxiously he had striven to maintain peace, and exactly defined England's attitude in certain possible contingencies.

The excitement all over the country was tremendous. The air was electrical with coming events, a spark would set the firmament ablaze. One could almost see the peoples of Russia, Germany, Austria, France, Belgium, and Serbia gaze questioningly, anxiously, across the Channel at the Island Kingdom, and wondering in that tense moment, What would England do?

Then flaring headlines in the press told that Liége, the great eastern fortress and arsenal of Belgium, had been furiously bombarded by the German artillery, and that Bethmann-Hollweg, the German Chancellor, had declared that a solemn treaty guaranteeing the neutrality of Belgium was of no more value than a scrap of paper.

Then England declared war against Germany, and on the 4th of August we knew that England was to take her place in the titanic world-war and step into the all-engulfing struggle.

So here it was at last. War with Germany! The restrained hostility of years was now no longer concealed, the long-pent-up passions were now let loose. Men seemed to breathe easier, and an air of relief pervaded the country.

England was like a sick man after a consultation with the surgeons. He looks eagerly and anxiously at the surgeons, hoping that no operation may be necessary, but dreading and expecting that it may. Once told by them that an operation is necessary in order that he may live, his doubts and hesitation disappear, and he agrees to submit and to undergo the drastic measures and emerge a strong and whole man. There is a relief that he has decided and the mind becomes tranquil.

The gravity of the issue was realised in England in those early August days. Those entitled to speak with authority pronounced that the war would be a big war—the greatest since the beginning of time—and that the men and women of our day and generation would have to pass through sorrow and tribulation and wade through dark and troubled waters before the end would be finally achieved.

The justness of England's quarrel was everywhere acknowledged, except in the land of the enemy, and the exposure of the tortuous and insidious German diplomacy stirred up the English sense of straight dealing and fairplay.

On 6th August I motored down from the Highlands to Edinburgh, through the Pass of Killiecrankie and some of the loveliest scenery in Scotland.

Everywhere were signs of mobilisation. Khaki soldiers and "mufti" recruits at every dépôt and around recruiting sergeants. The price of petrol had suddenly risen—why, nobody quite knew, but somebody was making money out of it, we were sure. At one town I paid ten shillings for a two-gallon tin.

In the evening I reached Queensferry, but was not allowed to cross at that hour. As the ferry would not be going again till next morning I motored back to Dunfermline, and having stopped the night there, returned early in the morning to the Ferry. This time I got across with my car. The Firth of Forth presented a very busy scene that morning. Torpedo boats and naval craft of all sorts and sizes were dashing about, and in the distance were the large dark outlines of big ships of war.

From Queensferry a rapid run brought me to Edinburgh, where the whole talk in hotel smoking-rooms, at table, and on the street, was of war. The kilted soldier was looked at with more interest as he walked the streets, and appeals were placarded on every prominent place for new recruits.

The morning papers announced that the House of Commons had passed a war vote of one hundred million pounds, and that Kitchener had asked for five hundred thousand men to join the army.

The Cabinet, like a good physician, was giving the nation its medicine in small doses during these early days. Doctors will tell you that small doses frequently repeated are so much better than a big dose taken at one wry mouthful, for a big heroic dose taken at one gulp often causes nausea. The hundred million pounds and the five hundred thousand men made the first teaspoonful of the national physic which was to help get rid of the fatty degeneration and change our sleeping, sluggish strength into the crouch and spring and hit of the prize fighter.

Next day I took train for London in order to offer my medical service to the War Office. There was an urgent demand for surgeons to volunteer for active service, and at this particular juncture good surgeons who were free to go were not very plentiful. As I was on a tour of surgical clinics at this time I decided to do my bit for the country and the men in the field. Having nothing to do when I reached London that evening, I strolled into a music hall and heard "God Save the King," "Rule, Britannia," the "Marseillaise," the Russian, Belgian, and Serbian national hymns—all blared out to cheering and shouting crowds, who seemed to thoroughly enjoy "being at war." It was reminiscent of the days of the Boer War in 1899:

"'ALEA JACTA EST'—THE DIE IS CAST."

Early next day I visited the Medical Department of the War Office at Whitehall, and volunteered as a surgeon with the Expeditionary Army to France. Two days afterwards the War Office sent me a note requesting me to call at the office and be examined to see if I was physically fit. So I did. The physical examination was carried out with amazing celerity, and I was handed on as "fit." The genial old army doctor appointed for this duty of examining his younger colleagues made his diagnosis on sight almost, and toyed easily with his stethoscope while he inquired about the state of the teeth and the digestion.

I was then ushered into another office and was duly appointed a Temporary Lieutenant in the Royal Army Medical Corps.

All the civilian surgeons accepted for service with the army—with the exception of a few consulting surgeons—were given the rank of Temporary Lieutenant. Seniority or special skill or previous war experience mattered nothing. I had already served as a Civil Surgeon, attached to the Royal Army Medical Corps during the South African War, and had a medal and four clasps from that campaign, and since that period had been surgeon to an important hospital in New Zealand, and was a retired Captain in the New Zealand Medical

Corps. That, however, did not entitle me to hold any higher rank than the young medical man who had completed his medical training only a week ago. Many able medical men all over the country had voluntarily left lucrative practices and important surgical and medical staff appointments in big London and provincial hospitals and were enrolled as Lieutenants in the Royal Army Medical Corps, on the same footing as junior medical men who had perhaps been their pupils but a few weeks before. We all ranked below the regular officers of the Royal Army Medical Corps. Volunteers for combatant commissions who had had previous experience were given rank accordingly. Some discrimination was made in the combatant arm, and rightly so. No discrimination was made in the medical service, and undoubtedly that was a mistake. The same lack of organised control was exhibited at every turn in the medical service. Men with imperfect professional skill and experience were given duties which should have been entrusted only to men fully possessed of those qualifications. This criticism is not merely a destructive one. Criticism is absolutely necessary at certain times, and there are some mistakes in policy which should be freely ventilated. This same policy was pursued by the Army Medical Department during the South African War, and was very openly discussed. This led to drastic changes in the organisation of the Royal Army Medical Corps, following on the Commission of Inquiry set up by Mr. Brodrick (now Lord Midleton). In this war, I regret to say, the old leaven has again appeared, and its re-appearance has aroused considerable comment and been a cause of inefficiency.

After having been given my commission I was told to procure a uniform—Sam Browne belt, a revolver, blankets, and other campaigning kit—and to be prepared to move in forty-eight hours. With great difficulty I managed to get some sort of equipment together. The military tailors were working at high pressure, and when asked to make a coat or breeches in a certain time simply said, "It can't be done." By skilful diplomacy I got a coat in one place, a pair of riding breeches in another, puttees at another, leggings elsewhere, and so on. One could not then obtain khaki shirts or ties in London. I did not get a revolver, although this was on the list of things necessary. Neither did I purchase a sword. Why a medical officer should be asked to carry a sword and a revolver, and at the same time wear a Red Cross brassard on the left arm, I am at a loss to understand. I have asked many senior medical officers of what use a revolver and sword were to a doctor on active service, and the only reply I could get was that they were useful to defend the wounded. It would have been much more sensible for the War Office to tell each medical officer to get several pairs of rubber gloves for dressings and operations. I sometimes wondered if the War Office expected the surgeons to perform amputations with a sword. However, I did not get a revolver, and I did not get a sword. Later on, in France, I have seen mild-looking young surgeons arrive at the front armed to the teeth, with swords, revolvers and ammunition, clanking spurs, map cases, field-glasses and compasses strung all round them, and on their left arm the brassard with the Red Cross. We called them " Christmas trees."

At last my equipment was complete, and I received orders to go to Aldershot and report to the Assistant Director of Medical Services for duty.

I was now a " Surgeon in Khaki " and part of that great military hammer—the British Expeditionary Force.

When I arrived at Aldershot the town seemed deserted. The majority of the big barracks were empty. We were told that the British Army had just left for the Continent, and that the Aldershot command, under General Haig, had gone to a man. Aldershot was rapidly preparing to receive and train recruits, mobilise reinforcements, and keep up a steady flow of men to replace casualties. This was great news. When we left London we did not know that the British Expeditionary Army had gone.

The A.D.M.S. (Assistant Director of Medical Services) put me on duty at the Cambridge Military Hospital at Aldershot, while awaiting orders for the front. Several surgeons awaiting orders were already here, and we all billeted at the Victoria Hotel. We were soon at work examining and passing recruits, inoculating troops against typhoid, and vaccinating all who had no conscientious objections. Some had " conscientious " objections to inoculation. Soldiers should not be allowed liberty of conscience in these matters. They should be made immune against typhoid and smallpox at "the word of command" in spite of the screechings of fanatics suffering from distorted cerebration.

Our duty at the recruiting dépôts was a very amusing one. We here came in contact with the first hopefuls of Kitchener's new army. The first call to arms generally brings in a very motley crowd. The best of the recruits do not turn up during the first few days, as these have generally some domestic or business matters to arrange. It was the "First Footers" we got in these days at Aldershot.

Another medical officer and myself took over one dépôt. We arrived at 8.30 a.m. Standing in a straggling two-deep line before the dépôt door were about three hundred men of the most variegated texture—some lean, some fat, some smart, some unkempt, but all looking very cheerful and hopeful. A smart R.A.M.C. sergeant is waiting at the door with a list of their names. It is our duty to examine physically this first batch of three hundred, to see if they are fit enough to train to fight Germans. Ten men are marched into the dépôt. Each doctor takes five at a time. At the word of command they strip and the doctor begins. He casts a professional eye rapidly over the nude recruit. A general look like this to a trained eye conveys a lot. The chest is examined, tongue, mouth, and teeth looked at. The usual sites for rupture are examined. About three questions are asked: "Any previous illness?" "Age?" "Previous occupation?" A mark is placed against the name, the nude Briton is told to clothe himself, and the examination is over. It is done at express speed, and although the examination is not very thorough it is sufficient to enable an experienced man to detect most physical defects. If a man passed, he was put down for foreign service. Some had slight defects and were put down for home defence. Some had glaring defects and were turned down altogether. We had all sorts of derelicts turn up. One weary-looking veteran, unwashed and with straw sticking in his hair, indicative of a bed in a haystack the previous night, was blind in one eye and very lame. A draper's assistant from a London shop had a twisted spine, an old soldier had syphilitic ulcers on the legs, some had bad hearts from excessive smoking, some bad kidneys from excessive drinking, some young men were really sexagenarians from hard living, and so on. They were old men before their time. The occupations of our recruits were as diverse as their shapes and constitutions —a runaway sailor, a Cockney coster, a draper's assistant, a sea cook, a medical student, a broken-down parson, an obvious gaolbird, and a Sunday-school teacher.

> " Cook's son, duke's son, son of a belted earl,
> Son of a Lambeth publican, they're all the same to-day."

Before the doctor the son of a prize fighter makes a better showing than the son of a consumptive bishop. We had orders not to be too strict with our physical examination. We were not to turn a man down if he could be usefully employed in any State service during the war. For instance, many of the " weeds " amongst the young men, the cigarette victims, the pasty-faced, flat-chested youths, those who had lived down dark alleys and in unhygienic surroundings all their lives, were all capable of being made into better men. Regular meals, plain food, good quarters, baths, cleanliness and hard work, marching, drilling and gymnastics, made these slouching, dull-eyed youths into active, smart men. They then held their heads up, breathed the free air, lost their sullenness, and became cheerful. Some of the recruits were not fit to be made into soldiers, and work could always be found for them. There are so many openings for the willing man at this time, be it cook's assistant, mess servant, officer's servant, orderly, or bootmaker's help.

It was always an interesting sight to see the sergeant and corporal drill these clumsy recruits, and show them how to walk, and where to place their feet. The army drill sergeant has a very caustic wit and a wonderful fund of cutting comments. He knows his audience well, and with a few crisp epithets can galvanise a sluggish recruit or a slouching company into something instinct with alertness.

On 21st August, six surgeons, including myself, were ordered to hold ourselves in readiness for service abroad. We were told to overhaul our kits thoroughly, think out all necessary things, and not to have any excessive baggage. None of us had. The Wolseley valise held our little all.

The last good-byes were said, and at 4 p.m. we entrained at Aldershot for our journey to " somewhere in France." We were all very glad to be off. We were all very curious to see and take part in the romance and adventures of the great battles that we knew would be sure to take place.

Romance! Adventure! Very soon we were up against cold facts, and there was no romance or pomp and circumstance then.

CHAPTER II.

LE HAVRE AND HARFLEUR.

At 12 p.m. we detrained at Southampton, hungry and thirsty. Owing to lack of foresight we had had nothing to eat since breakfast. The night was a beautiful one, and a voyage across channel sounded very inviting. We marched our 350 R.A.M.C. orderlies on to our transport, the *Braemar Castle,* and the officers tried to find a place to sleep. We managed to get some corners in the smoking-room, and curled up as best we could in the cramped places. The ship was packed full of troops, and we learned that we were the first reinforcements for the Expeditionary Army. We had two generals on board and the headquarter staff of a new division. Our destination was to be Le Havre. At 2 a.m. we steamed out, followed by several other transports crowded with soldiers. Torpedo-boat destroyers kept watchful eyes on us across channel, and twice a huge searchlight played all round us from far out at sea. The navy was watching on the deep waters. The soldiers on board slept on the deck, on hatches, anywhere, and they were all up and cheerfully carolling at dawn. When a soldier wakes his first thought is for food, and at 5 a.m. they were all discussing bully beef and biscuits.

The ship's cook had prepared cauldrons of tea,—and Tommy loves tea. One wag after breakfast stood on a hatch reciting, "Dearly beloved brethren, the Scripture moveth us in sundry places," to a congregation of grimy-faced soldiers.

At 12.30 midday we sighted Le Havre, and in two hours were tied alongside the wharf. The disembarkation rapidly followed, and at 4 p.m. we were on the march through Le Havre to our encampment. As we steamed into Le Havre there was a scene of the wildest enthusiasm, and the whole harbour front was a mass of cheering men and women and children. "Vive l'Angleterre!" "Vive Tommy!" "Vive l'entente cordiale!" Flags and handkerchiefs were waved from every window, and the picture of enthusiastic welcome was most inspiring. Our men seemed to thoroughly enjoy it, and cheered and yelled their throaty greetings as loudly and as heartily as the French. One would call in a bull voice, "Are we downhearted?" and the reply, "No!" from thousands of throats, echoed and reverberated over the sea front.

Then would come a piping voice, "Do we like beer?" followed by a unanimous roar of "Yes." The French welcome was a spontaneous and enthusiastic one, and Le Havre, gay with bunting and twined flags, shouted itself hoarse that day. I visited Le Havre some months later and saw a crowded British transport arrive. There was no cheering, no flags, no excitement. At the wharf was a big hospital ship, and wounded soldiers were being carried aboard by stretcher-bearers.

The French had, since August, passed through some days of disappointment and despair, and the German was still in France. The frenzied ecstasy of that welcome of August, the gifts of flowers, of fruit, of wine were no longer there, but deep down there was still the same welcome, unspoken but warm and sincere.

A dusty march of eight miles on a hot, blistering road brought us to our camp at Harfleur. We were indeed on historic ground. Close by were the remains of the old Castle of Harfleur that Henry V. and his men-at-arms stormed in the long ago.

On this same field Henry is said to have addressed his soldiers:

> " And you good yeomen,
> Whose limbs were made in England, show us here
> The mettle of your pasture; let us swear
> That you are worth your breeding."

It was on this field and at that time that old Bardolph said:

> " Would I were in an alehouse in London.
> I would give all my fame for a pot of ale and safety."

So here again, in the twentieth century, were some thousands of good yeomen whose limbs were made in England, and a pot of ale would have been relished by all, for the day had been a thirsty one.

Our arrival at camp was not expected. The commandant seemed very surprised to see us, but told us to make ourselves at home. We had no kits, no blankets, no tents, no food—all had been left on the wharf—and no hot water was procurable. We made

2

a meal off our "iron rations," which consist of a small waterproof cover holding a tin of bully beef, biscuits, pepper and salt and tea. Pipes were lit and we then lay down as we were, under the lee of a haystack, and slept till bugle-call, when we awoke, cold and damp with dew. The nights were very cold at this time and the days terribly hot.

The camp at Harfleur had about five or six thousand men, composed of representatives of all arms of the service—Highlanders, Guardsmen, Engineers, and details from dozens of other regiments. We were reinforcements. Rumours were coming through at this time that all was not well with our army, and we were disquieted to hear that it was being steadily pushed back and fighting desperately. The retirement of our army occasioned anxiety at Le Havre, our principal base at that time, and the reinforcements at Harfleur could not be joined up till the position became clearer.

At Harfleur we got little authentic news. We lived on rumours, and some of these were of the most extraordinary kind. There was one rumour that came through, and the Tommies fully believed it. It was said that the Germans cut off the right hand of every captured stretcher-bearer, and killed every prisoner of the combatant rank. Our men were quite determined to die fighting, and the stretcher-bearers asked for guns. The day after our arrival in camp we were given tents, and these were pitched in the morning. Twelve men were put to each tent, but blankets were few and we could only give four blankets to each tent. Next day the tents were struck and packed away for some unknown reason, and that night we all had to sleep in the open. The officers' kits arrived on the second day, and on the fourth day we were told to take from them only what was absolutely necessary. It was said that our kits were to be either packed away or burned. It was said also that the whole camp equipment, tents, blankets, etc., were to be burned. Later in the day this order was countermanded and we again took possession of our kits. We guessed from all these various orders that the position at the front was uncertain, and, as history has since shown, such was the case. On our fourth day at Harfleur a flying man arrived in his aeroplane from England, and we all crowded round to know what the latest news was. He had none to give, but told us that he had flown over a part of the German army. I think that he brought some important information, for that afternoon the whole camp was set to work digging trenches right across the front of the camp. We had more rumours of "tremendous British losses," "breakdown of French mobilisation," "stubborn fighting," but nothing authentic reached us.

However, work proceeded feverishly in the camp. Harfleur was on the main road leading from the north to Le Havre. It was said that the Germans were advancing, and this was true. A raiding force of 20,000 men—one German division—of cavalry, gunners, and infantry—the latter on fast motor-lorries—was certainly moving on Le Havre, and the intention was to destroy the British base dépôt, burn our huge stores, and capture and sink all the shipping and blow up the railways. Our camp was to delay this raid till the French could move up some divisions. Accordingly, lines of trenches were dug across the turnip fields and meadows. The farmhouses were surrounded by trenches and put into a state of defence. The doctors and stretcher-bearers were ordered to occupy an orchard about 500 yards in rear of the trenches. There was an extraordinary resemblance between one old farmhouse adjoining the camp and the famous farmhouse of Hougoumont at Waterloo. There was an old chapel in the centre of the farm, near to the big two-storied stone dwelling. Behind the chapel were the wine cellars and stables. To the right of the house was a long orchard surrounded by a stone wall about 5 feet high. The farmhouse and farmyard were surrounded by a high stone wall. Also there was a big gateway as at Hougoumont. Inside and lining the stone walls were tall pine trees. Our men soon began to make some alterations in the quaint old Norman place. The lower branches of the trees were lopped off. Trenches were made inside the stone wall and stones were pulled out of the base for loopholes for rifles, so that our men could lie in the ditch and fire through the bottom of the wall. The same thing was done in the orchard, and men of the Rifle Brigade were told off to line its walls when the time came. This farm, if exposed to artillery, of course would have been a death-trap, but against infantry or cavalry would have been a very hornet's nest for the enemy to attack. The gateways were pulled down, barricades were placed across the gaps, and machine-guns controlled the angles and were able to sweep the open spaces, should a rush be made, with a hail of lead.

All was ready for a second Hougoumont, and the picture was completed by the old farmer's wife, who was ordered to leave the farm, but who firmly refused to budge. Had the Germans come, like her ancient prototype on that June day at Waterloo, she would most likely have taken shelter at the foot of the cross in the chapel.

But the Germans did not come, and history is deprived of a moving and stirring story.

It was tragic but ludicrous to see the blank despair and consternation on the face of the old farmer when we started to lop down some of his trees, dig trenches round his farm and through his turnip fields. Knowing very little about the war, and only vaguely interested in the invasion of France, he was deeply concerned about his turnips and his trees. Everything, however, was put right for him before we left.

When all our preparations for defence were complete two German aeroplanes passed over us going towards Le Havre. Here they were fired on, and they then returned to have a further look at Harfleur and circled slowly over our camp. As we had no aircraft guns they descended fairly low, and I think must have seen everything there was to see. We had field-glasses out and could easily discern the black cross painted on the wings of the Taube.

So there we were in our trenches commanding the roads to Le Havre, with a Hougoumont and an orchard, and stone walls lined with riflemen. History, so far, has not recorded how we "held the gate" to Le Havre without firing a shot and without losing a man, but I am sure that it was our preparations, seen by the enemy aeroplanes, that deterred the Germans from coming on. It was a raiding German force, and a raiding force has no time to tackle defences and strongly held positions. A brigade of French cavalry moved across our front and rode as a big cavalry screen towards the advancing raiders. Fifteen thousand French troops followed them; and when twelve miles from our camp the Germans turned back, the menace was over, and we breathed again.

A fast scouting motor-car containing three Prussian officers ran headlong into a barricade cleverly placed across a road about ten miles from Harfleur. A ditch, broad but shallow, was made across the road near a curve, and artfully concealed with gravel laid on thin planking across the top. The car rushed right on to this and was upset. Some concealed French cavalry then rode up and captured the party.

The French officer who made the capture told me that the German officers were livid with anger when he and his men rode up with drawn sabres. One of the German officers had a revolver in his hand, which he flung violently at the head of the chauffeur.

This defence of the road at Harfleur was one of those minor incidents of the war which has been forgotten or ignored in the swirl of the big happenings at that time. The situation of Le Havre and Harfleur was then one of grave peril and gave rise to considerable anxiety. One need not have been on the spot to grasp the dangerous possibilities. Our defence of Harfleur ended tamely. We were told one day that Lord Kitchener was at Le Havre and had ordered the evacuation of the big base by the British. That night we were ordered by our commandant to strike the camp, move into Le Havre, and embark on transports for a destination unknown.

The day before we left Le Havre some British stragglers from our retreating army turned up in camp. About twenty-five dirty, grimy, footsore men, with unkempt hair and stubbly beards, wandered in and told us that they had lost their regiments and their way after Mons. Since then they had been gipsying through France towards the coast. Sometimes they got a lift on a farmer's cart, but mostly they walked. They said that the French people had treated them very well, and they certainly did not look hungry. As usual, they told most harrowing tales. One man said that the whole army had been captured by an army of twenty million Germans!

On the morning of our last day at Harfleur we were all thrilled by the visit of a German spy. I have said previously that when the trenches were being dug at Harfleur the medical detachment was sent to an orchard in the rear. A road led past the gate of this orchard. At the gateway we had two of our men on sentry-go. Farther down the road was a French sentry with a fixed bayonet. At 3 a.m. a powerful two-seater automobile dashed up this road and pulled up at the gateway. The driver had on a heavy khaki motor overcoat and a khaki cap. His face was muffled in a khaki scarf. An officer, also in khaki, stepped out and began questioning our men at the gate. He asked how many men were in the camp; were there any big guns, and where were they? Had any ammunition been brought up that day? Our sentries were heavy north-countrymen, recently enlisted, and did not tumble to the fact that it was an unusual thing for a British officer to put such questions to a private on sentry-go. The officer then got on his car and went back in the direction of Le Havre. We were all agreed that the strange officer was a spy dressed up to look like a British officer. The French told us that Le Havre was full of spies at this time, and that they had made many arrests of suspects.

CHAPTER III.

FROM LE HAVRE TO THE BAY OF BISCAY.

WE knew that serious events must have happened when K. of K. had personally visited Le Havre and had ordered its evacuation. It was Napoleon who said that it was a disastrous thing to attempt to change an army's base during the actual progress of a war. But in this war old maxims and trite sayings go by the board. Anyone having the most elementary knowledge of war, and what an army in the field signifies, will agree that even if changing a base may not lead to disaster, it is nevertheless a very formidable and a very risky move. Le Havre at this time was a huge base from which our army in the field was receiving its supplies. Transports conveying all the necessaries for a fighting army unloaded their cargoes on its wharves. From there the supplies were sent by train to the advanced base in the centre of France, and from there onward to the various refilling stations. The destruction of Le Havre, or its temporary loss as a base, would have been a calamity. The army would have ceased to receive food, waggons, ammunition and equipment, guns, horses, forage, reinforcements, hospital supplies, etc. An army without ammunition and food is no longer of any fighting value. Think also of the quantities of material necessary to supply an army of 70,000 men, and this will give some idea of the immense war dépôt Le Havre was at this time. Circumstances must have indeed been serious to have necessitated a change of base. It meant also that the railway arrangements so carefully thought out, and which had so far been in operation, would have to be suddenly changed. Supply trains would have to be sent to the front from some other base, and returning empty supply trains and hospital trains would have to be diverted from Le Havre to the place chosen as the future base. The task was a gigantic one, and was rendered more so because it had to be completed in a hurry.

We reached Le Havre from Harfleur in the late afternoon. A large convoy of Belgian ambulances full of wounded was moving through the streets towards the wharves, and a French Infantry Division passed us in full panoply of war going east. Six large transports with steam up were lying at the wharves. The wharves were a scene of unparalleled activity, and when one got right down amidst this activity and looked around, one could realise that things were very chaotic. Every one was shouting and cursing; contradictory orders were given; some stores which had just been loaded in one of the holds of one transport were being again unloaded. Through careless handling a huge crate of iron bedsteads for a military hospital fell into the sea between the ship and the wharf. But as the stores were Government property—therefore nobody's property—no one seemed to mind very much. The stage between the ship and the big sheds was packed with all sorts of goods in inextricable confusion. Here were bales of hospital blankets dumped on kegs of butter, there boxes of biscuits lying packed in a corner, with a forgotten hose-pipe playing water on them. Inside the sheds were machine-guns, heavy field pieces, ammunition, some aeroplanes, crowds of ambulance waggons, London buses, heavy transport waggons, kitchens, beds, tents for a general hospital, stacks of rifles, bales of straw, mountainous bags of oats, flour, beef, potatoes, crates of bully beef, telephones and telegraphs, water carts, field kitchens, unending rolls of barbed wire, shovels, picks, and so on. All had been brought into the sheds and left there in a higgledy-piggledy fashion. An Army Service man was trying in despair to get some forage on board; a colonel of the Medical Staff was trying to get his Base Hospital on board. There was apparently no *single* brain in control, and the loading of the ships went on in the most extraordinary way. Things nearest the ship's side were put in first. Part of a Base Hospital was put in with part of a Battery, followed by bundles of compressed straw fodder and boxes of soap.

The transport *Turcoman* was full of troops. There seemed to be thousands of them on board, and the decks were packed with men. On walking up the gangway I was met by the officer commanding the troops, and he told me that I could not be allowed on board with any men as the ship was already overcrowded. I told him that my orders were to embark on the *Turcoman*, but the reply, "Very sorry indeed, but it can't be done," settled the matter.

So I descended, and with difficulty picked my way along another wharf and found another transport, the *Cestrian*, also a centre of the same scene of bustle and activity as the *Turcoman*. The *Cestrian* was crowded with soldiers, and was being frantically loaded up with all sorts of goods, from aeroplanes to bandages.

I got my men on board and told them to make themselves as comfortable as they could on deck, and after some searching round at last found a corner of the smoking-room which would serve me for a bed for the night. Here my servant dumped down my valise.

I was unable to find out the destination of the *Turcoman*; nobody seemed to know, but there were rumours that it was to be "somewhere in the Bay of Biscay." Nobody knew where the *Cestrian* was going. As my orders were to travel by the *Turcoman*, and as I was really on the *Cestrian*, I was anxious to find out if the destination of the two boats was to be the same port. But nobody could tell me, so I lit my pipe of tobacco, leaned over the ship's side, and never troubled any more about my orders. I really did not know whether the *Cestrian* was going to England or another part of France, or the Black Sea for that matter.

The scene on the *Cestrian* was a strange one. It was now quite dark and the loading of the cargo was carried out under electric flares. There were on board 2600 soldiers and 600 horses. These unfortunate horses had been put on board twenty-four hours before the troops embarked, instead of the other way about, and the smell from the hot, stifling horse-boxes was overpowering. Why these poor beasts were not embarked last of all, was a mystery. Imagine 600 horses cooped up in narrow boxes during a long, hot, stifling summer day, when they could easily have been kept at the horse dépôt close by till the last minute!

One horse died before we started, and was slung out by ropes on to the wharf.

This horse episode was the occasion of much scathing comment amongst senior officers and old cavalry and artillery non-coms.

It is a pity that some of the higher command—those responsible—could not have heard the remarks of these knowing old non-commissioned officers.

At last the ship's holds were full. Gangways were up and we dropped slowly down the locks to the Seine mouth, and so out into the Channel. We were met by a fierce, gusty head wind and welcomed it for the horses' sakes. Large wind ventilators were arranged to allow the fresh air to reach the horse-boxes.

Our men slept on the decks, and there were so many of them that to step one's way over them would have been almost impossible.

The dining-rooms, cabins, and smoking-rooms were full of sleeping or dozing officers. I managed to commandeer an old sofa cushion, and lay on that in the corner of the smoking-room and went to sleep, and dreamt of thousands of horses looking reproachfully at me out of boxes.

At break of day we were all up at bugle-call and soon washed. The ship's cook was a man of some eminence in his profession, for he had provided porridge and milk, ham and eggs, bread and butter and tea for our breakfast, and, filled with amazement, we sat round to enjoy it. Generally of meals on a transport there are none. A big cruiser was seen after breakfast to be bearing rapidly down on us, and the usual " optimist " present, after carefully observing her through a telescope, pronounced her nationality as German, and that it was now a watery grave in the Bay of Biscay for 2600 men and 600 horses. As she came nearer we showed our flag, and she displayed the French ensign. We gave her our number and dipped our bit of bunting, and the great ironclad sheered off. It was a relief to know that she was about, and looking after our transports.

On the way out from Le Havre we passed the United States battleship *Tennessee*, and our men seeing some of her sailors standing in a group gazing at us, gave a cheer and the usual " Are we downhearted ? No ! " greeting. The American sailors gave a real good hearty cheer, and yells of " good luck "; but an officer then ran up to them and said something, and they became suddenly silent, and only waved their hands. They had probably been told by their officer that they were " neutrals," and belonged to the battleship of a nation friendly to all the belligerents. But we knew that they were with us " inside," and anyhow the Americans have not been neutral in their hearts. They are all " for us " and " for the Allies."

Life on board our transport was uneventful. We smoked and slept and ate. There was no room to walk about. I never saw such a crowded ship.

We had on board the complete *personnel* of a Base Hospital, and the medical officer commanding told me that he had orders to pitch his hospital at once at Nantes in order to take in wounded, as there was a big demand for more beds. In spite of his utmost endeavours he could not get his hospital equipment on the *Cestrian*.

All the instruments, dressings, and X-ray apparatus had been left behind for another boat, and he thought that he might not be able to get them for another week, or perhaps longer.

This was but another example of the lack of control at Le Havre during the change of base; a hospital was badly wanted at Nantes; all the *personnel* and half the equipment were sent away, and the other half left on the wharves. We learned later that the holds of our boat the *Cestrian* were not full when she left Le Havre, but that she had been ordered to leave on account of the horses being in such a bad state from the hot, stifling atmosphere in their quarters below decks.

It was necessary to proceed to sea to get a current of cold air down the ventilating shafts to the horses' cribs. This senseless blundering over the horses led to the death of several of the poor beasts, and besides crippled a Base Hospital at a time when it was urgently needed. Over and over again during this war one has met with instances of a want of reasoned judgment on the part of senior controlling officers. In certain emergencies they have been unable to " orientate " themselves—to use an Americanism—or to " envisage " a situation.

Blunders, slips, miscalculations, carelessness, in time of war mean the loss of valuable lives. We want alert, clear-brained, thinking men in all responsible posts. If a senior officer shows himself lacking in these essentials —then he must go. Many of the responsible French army officials at the beginning of the campaign proved themselves lacking in initiative and judgment. Joffre sent these officers to " Limoges." We should send our incapables to " Stellenbosch." Both places are indicative of a quiet retirement, where they can live without thinking, where there are quiet clubs, cigars and cocktails, and comfortable chairs for an afternoon nap. The good ship *Cestrian* was a very fine steamer, but a very dirty one at this epoch. She badly wanted a clean-up. The lavatories and water-closets were indescribably filthy and foul, and acrid ammoniacal fumes permeated the ship. No attempt was made at ordinary cleanliness, and no disinfectants were employed. Words could hardly describe the appallingly filthy state of the urinals and closets. It would have been so very simple to have made things cleaner. A sanitary squad could have been arranged in a few minutes to keep these places tidy and to maintain some control. But what was every one's business was nobody's business, and nothing was done during the three days and nights we were at sea.

As our ship approached the mouth of the Loire we

saw three large transports ahead of us and four more were following up behind. We slowly steamed through the narrow lock entrance to St. Nazaire and, after the usual delay in getting alongside, finally tied up to the wharf. The day was stiflingly hot and dusty, and we were glad to leave our ship and get on shore. The horses were at once unloaded, and very bad the poor beasts looked. It was pleasant, however, to see them, once they were on land, looking round and neighing with evident pleasure.

The troops were marched out to a large field or a dry salt marsh some few miles out of town. A rest camp or camp for army details was being rapidly arranged, and areas were being marked out for the various units,—gunners, engineers, and infantry regiments, and there was considerable bustle. No tents had yet arrived and the camp was quite exposed. Fortunately, the weather was good and sleeping out was no hardship. I reported my arrival to the camp commandant, and he said that he did not know where I had to go or what I had to do. He told me to "wait round and see what turned up." At this period one's arrival was always unexpected. We always got a smile of welcome and were always told to "wait round." There was never any demonstrative hurry. John Bull on the job doesn't make much fuss. I think that he does not make enough. As there was nothing to do apparently, and as nobody seemed to want me, I strolled back to the city of St. Nazaire and had afternoon tea in a pleasant café.

As I was leaving the café I met the A.D.M.S.

(Assistant Director of Medical Services). He asked me what duty I was on. I told him that I had just arrived and had reported my arrival, and was really wondering myself why I was at St. Nazaire. The A.D.M.S. said, "We are wanting medical officers urgently at the front. Would you please come with me." On our way to the office he explained that "the medical service had received some losses—casualties and missing, that there were a lot of wounded and a lack of hospital necessaries." He asked me if I had any "bandages, wool, or lint with me." I had none, of course, and the A.D.M.S. said that he had none to spare for the front. I thought of the Base Hospital on the *Cestrian* landed with only half its equipment, and of what a wonderful nation we are, and what a magnificent organiser John Bull is when he is really "on the job."

I received written orders from the A.D.M.S. to proceed by train at 4 a.m. next day to Le Mans, and report arrival and await orders there. Le Mans was the "advanced base" of the British army. I learned here also that our gallant army was retreating towards Paris, and fighting stubbornly against overwhelming numbers of Germans flushed with victory, and I was very glad to get orders to join up with my countrymen and get a chance of "doing my bit" also.

CHAPTER IV.

FROM THE BAY OF BISCAY TO EAST OF PARIS.

AFTER having received these definite orders I got my kit again conveyed to the *Cestrian* transport and slept that night in my old corner of the smoking-room. At 2.45 a.m. the surgeons detailed to join the army were up. A hasty cup of coffee and an apology for a wash—and we were down the ship-side, and on the way to the *gare*. The railway station at St. Nazaire at this time looked quite picturesque in the early morning. Its platforms were covered with straw, and rows of sleeping French soldiers lay comfortably around, while a stolid Grenadier sentry stood propped against the wall. There is no hurry at a French military station. The train was timed to start at 4 a.m., but that did not matter. At 5 a.m. it was quite ready. "C'est la guerre."

There were five of us travelling together—all medical officers—two Scotchmen, one Irishman, one Englishman, and one New Zealander. A very gruff Railway Transport officer gave me a military pass for the party. This gave us permission, we noticed, to travel to Paris viâ Le Mans. The pass was signed by the French authorities, but we were never asked to show it again.

The khaki uniform proclaimed we were British, the Sam Browne belt and stars showed we were officers, and the red-cross brassards on our left arms indicated our particular line of business. As the train moved off we wished our Railway Transport officer—an Englishman—a good morning, but this seemed to offend him, for he glared at us. Our Irish surgeon remarked that all Railway Transport officers were queer fish and very unpopular. Perhaps their particular specialty makes them so, but I have never heard an R.T.O. referred to in any other but denunciatory terms. A sanguinary adjective is always prefixed to the mystic trinity R.T.O. It is said that they lead unhappy lives and generally die of long, lingering illnesses. We soon settled down comfortably in our luxurious first-class carriage and tried to get to know each other. No very difficult task amongst doctors, who are generally most sociable animals. One of us was a specialist in fevers and had passed most of his days in typhoid and scarlet fever wards. One was a neurologist, with pronounced views on the power of suggestion in treating cases of incipient insanity. One was a pure physician, who said that the surgeons were not men of science but merely craftsmen, and were too fond of using the knife.

The surgeons, as became their calling, treated all criticism with good-humoured complaisance. We talked a lot about the duties of the doctor in this war, and we were all very curious to know the rôle played by a doctor when he was attached to a cavalry regiment, to a battery, or to a field ambulance. None of us knew very much about it, but we all were agreed that we had somehow to get alongside Mr. Thomas Atkins when he was wounded in battle, get him to a safe place, and give him of our best. Curiously enough, although we were all scattered later on to various units of different divisions, I met all my fellow-travellers again one time or another in the firing line. One of the Scotchmen I met just as he came out from under heavy shrapnel fire, and I asked him how he liked it. His reply is not printable. One I met in a field ambulance later with sleeves rolled up and busy dressing the wounds of a crowd of men just brought in from the firing line. One I met in a town in northern France looking cold and wet and miserable, and asked him also how he liked the war. He gave an expressive shrug. I have not met anyone yet who liked the war, except artillery officers.

Our train travelled slowly from St. Nazaire along the Loire to the capital city of Nantes. This charming city is situated on the banks of the delightful river. We had a lot of khaki and French soldiers on board the train, and as usual they fraternised well together. Tommy Atkins gets on amazingly well with the French piou-piou, and the French grenadier chaffs Tommy a lot and enjoys his company. When they get together they exchange caps for a time. This is a sign of unalterable friendship.

To see a French Cuirassier wearing a khaki cap and a Highlander in kilts wearing a Cuirassier's casque with its flowing horsetails always excited the merriment and loud " vives " of the French people. The kilts of our Highlanders are also greatly admired by the French. They were consumed with curiosity to know if the Scotchmen wore any trousers under them. Khaki was a great novelty along the Loire valley at this time, and our appearance roused tremendous enthusiasm and applause. At Nantes the good people brought us baskets of apples, and little French flags which we duly stuck on our coats or caps and wore till the train steamed out of the station.

Crowds of people rushed down to the railway platform to see us and cheer us on our way. Tommy's " Are we downhearted ? " and its stentorian " No ! " had a very optimistic sound, and the French liked it.

At Angers the train stopped two hours, and the officers strolled round the town. The men were not allowed off the platform. Angers, the ancient capital of the old Counts of Anjou, is a delightfully sleepy city. A princess of Anjou was in the long ago a Queen of England, and a fine statue to her memory stands in the centre of the town. It was dressed with an intertwined Union Jack and the Tricolor when we were there.

The old castle of Angers, with its deep moat and castellated towers, has withstood the ravages of centuries and is one of the finest examples of mediæval military masonry. Our walk through this city excited considerable comment and notice. It was Sunday, and a big congregation just leaving church stopped to stare at us and possibly to wonder why khaki was in

Angers. As we passed a café crowded with loungers sipping wine and coffee at the little tables on the street, all stood up to look at us. We felt very embarrassed and did not much like the novel experience, so sat round a small table ourselves, and while drinking our wine turned round to look at the people also. A French colonel caught our eye, and one of our party held a glass towards him, saying, "Vive la France!" The effect was theatrical: all jumped up, and lifting their glasses shouted, "Vive l'Angleterre!" "Vive l'entente cordiale!" Several French officers and citizens with ladies pulled up their chairs to our table, and we all drank wine very sociably together. One of our party of surgeons had been educated as a youth in Belgium and was an excellent French linguist. The people were all very anxious to hear the latest news. We had none to give except that large British reinforcements were coming over, and that England was now fairly on the job. In these early days of the war, when everything in France was "electrical," such sentiments were always cheerfully received. We drank a good many toasts before we left, and had our photographs taken three times. Just before the train started crowds of gentlemen and ladies, old and young, shook hands with us in the usual French way, with the left hand as often as the right. One beautiful and sparkling little French lady embarrassed one of us by a sudden warm embrace and a sisterly kiss on the cheek. The surprise of the khaki man was only momentary, and the lady, in return, was well and truly kissed on the lips. We were all sorry to leave

Angers, the city was charming, the wine was excellent and the people were most entertaining.

After Angers we had a long and dreary night ride to Le Mans. One curious incident occurred during the night. Our train was pulled into a siding at a small station and held there for three hours. At the end of this time a train, made up of forty-one huge locomotive engines, thundered by at sixty miles an hour going south. We were told that these were Belgian engines sent south to escape capture by the Germans.

In the cold shiver of a dark morning we bundled out at Le Mans, and at once made a dash for the railway buffet and got hot coffee and rolls. I then found my way with some difficulty in the darkness to the quarters of the A.D.M.S., to whom I had to report our arrival. He was in bed when I arrived, but got up and took my report. As usual he was surprised to know we were coming, and our visit was naturally an unexpected pleasure. He told us that we should have gone right on to Paris, as surgeons were badly wanted with the army which was retreating on to Paris. We were always being told that doctors were urgently required and were always delayed. We had definite orders to get out at Le Mans and report. The orders were in writing. No one was more anxious than we were to push rapidly on, and we chafed at the continual delays. The A.D.M.S. could not tell us when we would be able to get away from Le Mans as the train service was erratic. We were advised to "hang about the railway station" till "some train" started for the front. As this was highly unsatisfactory, I tried to find out how matters stood myself.

The stationmaster did not know when a train would start for Paris, as the line was blocked farther on by the military mobilisation. I found out, however, that a supply train conveying provisions and supplies for our men was to leave from Maroc some time during the day. Maroc was a small siding five miles from Le Mans. Here trains were made up for the various Army Corps. Maroc is a desert of sand and a truly desolate spot. We got our kits and a box of medical supplies—obtained with great difficulty at Le Mans—conveyed to this miniature Morocco, and we camped on the sand under the doubtful shade of the only two trees the place possessed, till 4 o'clock that afternoon. The only excitement was seeing a huge locomotive run off the track and block shunting operations for two hours. At last our huge supply train was ready. We all got into an empty guard's van and disposed our valises in the various corners. Two officers of the Royal Flying Corps joined us here and found accommodation in a waggon loaded with bags of wheat. We all clubbed together for mess, and laid in a stock of sardines, bread, butter, and a dozen bottles of red wine and cider. We learned from our flying friends that the army was retiring every day, and was supposed to be making for Paris.

We got some definite news for the first time of our big engagements at Mons, Landrecies, and Le Cateau, and how our army was furiously attacked and compelled to fall back, and that although the retirement at first was precipitate it soon became ordered and steady. We were also told that there were over 15,000 casualties, and that the medical arrangements had quite broken down. However, we had a sublime faith in our own countrymen, and knew that they would come out all right, somehow, somewhere.

At daybreak our train reached Tours, and at Blois we had a welcome wash and a decent cup of coffee. Our quarters in the guard's van had been most cramped and uncomfortable, and we were all anxious to leave the old tortoise of a train. At midday we passed through Orleans, and here French officers told us that the Germans were advancing on Paris, and in spite of prodigious losses were hacking their way through by weight of numbers and numberless batteries of artillery. We were told that the British army was to form part of the garrison of Paris, that Paris was fully prepared for a long siege, and that President Poincaré and the Government were at Bordeaux. All these rumours gave rise to keen discussions, and they certainly helped to while the time away in our dreary old van.

During the night we passed through Paris, and at break of day pulled up at the railway siding of Coulommiers.

The railway siding was full of ambulance trains, British and French. All the trains were filled with recently wounded men, and we got our first information that we were close to the actual scene of fighting. One French medical officer had rigged up a small dressing station on the station platform. An upturned box held his dressings, instruments, and antiseptics, and he had about twenty-five wounded Frenchmen all round him patiently waiting their turn. Most of them were slight cases, for the serious ones had already been put aboard the hospital trains.

Coulommiers at this time was the refilling point for the Army Service Corps, and our supply train was emptied here.

CHAPTER V.

THE ADVANCE TO THE MARNE.

Coulommiers at this time looked a little bit *dégagé*. It had been occupied by the Germans some days previously, and now the British had it. The French inhabitants were in Paris. The narrow old streets looked very cheerful and inviting when I passed through, for our Army Service men had several fires merrily blazing at the side of the *pavé*, and the smell of frying bacon and roasting coffee beans was inviting and appetising. Signs of the German occupation were everywhere apparent. Round the ashes of their fires in the side streets and square were the charred remains of old and valuable furniture—a carved leg of an old chair, a piece of the frame of a big mirror, a bit of a door, and so on. I think the German soldier enjoyed the novel sensation of cooking his food over burning cabinets and tables and chairs made in the times of the Louis' of France. Our men were extremely careful to avoid damage to French property and made their fires of chopped wood logs. Tommy has good feelings and is always a gentleman, and he genuinely pitied the French in their despoiled towns.

My orders were to report to the Principal Medical

Officer of the 5th Division of the 2nd Army. I could not find out where the 5th Division headquarters was, but ascertained that the 2nd Army headquarters was at the small hamlet of Doui, three miles away. My next problem was how to get there with my kit. Luckily, I found a motor-car driver about to start for the headquarters and he offered me a lift. This driver was one of the many gentlemen of leisure who had volunteered for service at the beginning of the war. He took out his own car at first and it broke down during the retreat, so he abandoned it by the roadside and got another car, the driver of which had been killed. We set off from Coulommiers at a rattling pace and passed part of the 3rd Division on the way. The headquarters of General Smith-Dorrien, the Commander of the 2nd Army, was a little cluster of houses by the roadside, and when we arrived the whole staff were standing by the road, while the grooms stood near holding their horses. Smith-Dorrien with another staff officer was poring over a map and indicating some spot on it with his finger. The Principal Medical Officer, Colonel Porter of the Army Medical Staff, now Surgeon-General Porter, was just coming out of a cottage, and I walked up, saluted, and reported my arrival. The Colonel gave me a cheery greeting, asked if I had breakfasted, and noticing the South African War ribbon on my tunic, said that as I had seen service before I would soon be quite at home. He asked me where I came from, and when told that it was New Zealand, inquired if the trout-fishing was still good. New Zealand seems to be principally known in England for its excellent trout streams.

I was then told to report to the officer commanding a section of the 15th Field Ambulance, which was lying about 500 yards farther down the road. I reported to Major O—— of the Royal Army Medical Corps, who told me that he was waiting to evacuate some wounded to Coulommiers before moving up to rejoin the headquarters of the ambulance which was advancing with the 15th Infantry Brigade. There were sixteen wounded British in a small farmhouse beside the road. They were lying on straw on the floor and the wounds of all of them had been dressed. When I entered they were drinking milk supplied by the old farmer and his wife. This old farmhouse had been occupied by the Germans two days previously, and the old farmer brought me through the house to show what the Huns had done. His two wooden bedsteads had been smashed. All his wife's clothes had been taken out of a chest of drawers and torn up, and the chest had been battered badly with an axe. The windows were broken and two legs of the kitchen table had been chopped off. An old family clock lay battered in a corner, and an ancient sporting gun was broken in two. The farmer showed me one of his wife's old bonnets which had been thrown into the fire by these lovely Germans and partially burned. Fancy burning an old woman's bonnet! All the fowls and chickens had been killed. Two German soldiers got into the fowlyard and struck all the birds down with their bayonets. A fine Normandy dog lay dead at the garden gate, shot by a German non-commissioned officer because the poor beast barked at him.

The old-fashioned furniture and adornments of the house had been destroyed. All of the pictures were broken except two—one of these was a framed picture of Pope Leo XIII., and the other was one representing the Crucifixion. We guessed that the German troops must have been Bavarians, who are mostly Catholic.

I have described this wrecked home as it was typical of hundreds of others that I have seen in France. It all seemed so stupid, so senseless, so paltry, and mean. Conceive the frightfulness of burning an old lady's bonnet and smashing an old clock that had been in the family's possession for three generations, and had ticked the minutes to the farmer's folk and whose face had been looked at by those long since dead. The old farmer was in tears and very miserable. He said that the German soldiers were very drunk and had brought a lot of bottles of champagne with them, round which they spent a very hilarious night. One of the men had a very fine voice and sang a German drinking song, whilst the others hiccuped the chorus. There were certainly a lot of empty champagne bottles lying about, and I don't think that the old farmer's beverage ever soared above *vin rouge*, so the bottles must have been German loot.

About eleven o'clock, while we were still waiting for returning empty supply waggons to take off our wounded, we heard that some German prisoners were being marched in. This caused some excitement, and, speaking for myself, I was consumed with curiosity to see some specimens of this great German army and observe what manner of men they were. Under a strong guard of cavalry three hundred prisoners with about ten officers were marched into a field close to our farmhouse. It was laughable to see our old farmer. He rushed frantically up the road, his eyes blazing with excitement and joy, and stood gazing at his country's enemies with an expression of malicious joy and delight.

I was struck with the appearance of these prisoners. They were very tired, absolutely done in, and marched along the road with a most bedraggled and weary step. Were these the men who had goose-stepped through Belgium's stately capital and had pushed the united armies of France and England before them in one of the most rapid marches in history? They were utterly broken down with fatigue, and their famished expression and wolfish eyes betokened the hardships they had recently undergone. When they were halted in the field they simply rolled on to the ground from sheer exhaustion. On looking closer, however, one could see that they were fine soldiers, athletic, well-built, lean, wiry fellows, with shaven heads and prominent features, slim-waisted and broad-shouldered, clothed in smart, well-fitting, bluish-grey uniforms, well-shod with good serviceable boots, each with a light water-bottle clipped to his belt and a haversack over the shoulder; certainly no fault could be found with them as specimens of muscular and active soldiery.

The officers, disdaining to show fatigue, sat by themselves in a group apart and smoked pipes and cigarettes. The famished men were supplied with British bully beef and biscuits, and buckets of water were brought to them for drink. They at once threw off their exhaustion and simply rushed the food. We realised that they had been marched to a stop, and that the commissariat of that particular Army Corps must have broken down. The augury was a good one. Amongst them were some slightly wounded men—principally hand, scalp, and face wounds. These we dressed, and the men seemed very grateful to the medical officers for what was done. One of my men, with a slight shrapnel wound of the wrist, after I had dressed and bandaged it, seized my hand and kissed it. That is the German way, perhaps, but un-British, and I do not love things German or un-British to-day. One of the men had a slight wound, but a very painful one owing to a small shell splinter sticking on to a nerve. Lieut. M'C—— administered a few whiffs of chloroform while I extracted the fragment of iron. Poor M'C—— remarked to me that this was the first anæsthetic that he had administered during the war, although he had been through the whole retreat from Mons, and that it was for a German. I say poor M'C——; this splendid young doctor was killed later on in Flanders while gallantly attending wounded in the trenches under a hellish shrapnel fire. This group of prisoners belonged to the Jägers of the Prussian Guard, one of the best infantry units in the German Army. We were all very pleased that they had been bagged, and I don't think that they worried much about it themselves. The officers, however, seemed very sullen—that also pleased us.

Shortly after the arrival of the Guard Jägers some empty motor supply waggons, returning from the front, were stopped. We packed plenty of straw on them and put our wounded British and Germans comfortably on top, and sent them all off to the hospital train at Coulommiers. Then our commanding officer, Major O——, gave the order to our ambulance drivers to harness up the horses and prepare to trek. We knew that our army was making a stand at last, and that the long retreat from Belgium was over.

All the morning heavy firing was heard on our front towards the river Marne, and we were not sure what was happening. We knew that our cavalry was at work somewhere, for the Guard Jägers had been bagged by our horsemen, but more than that we did not know. However, we were soon on the road, and following Napoleon's maxim to his Generals—always to march on the firing. The roads were terribly dusty, the day was hot and sultry, and a blazing sun beat mercilessly down upon us. We all cursed our caps, and certainly the present khaki cap supplied to our officers and men deserves a curse. It gives no protection to the head or neck in summer, and in rainy weather it is soon soaked.

Marching on foot behind lumbering ambulance waggons on a dusty road, and under a hot sun, is no picnic. Eyes get full of dust, throat gets parched, feet get hot, and the khaki uniform wraps round one like a sticky blanket. So for many miles we marched, and all the time the sound of the guns became more and more distinct and intense. We passed St. Ouen and by St. Cyr, and at 4.30 o'clock we seemed to be in the centre of the artillery thunder area. Great guns were screeching and roaring all round us, and some of the enemy's shells were bursting to our left front near the road along which we were moving. We were then ordered to pull our waggons off the road and bivouac them under a clump of trees near at hand in order to conceal them from enemy aeroplanes, which were hovering high up in the blue. The reason for at times concealing a Field Ambulance is that when a column is on the march the Field Ambulance has a definite position in the column; generally it is behind the ammunition column. The ambulance waggons, with their big white tented covers and conspicuous red crosses, are often the most prominent features on the road. The enemy flying-man when he sees a Field Ambulance knows that there is at least a brigade consisting of four battalions and an ammunition column in front of it, and he can then direct his gunners to plant their shells in front of the ambulance and so get the ammunition column and the brigade. Hence the necessity for sometimes hiding the whereabouts of a Field Ambulance.

After we had bivouacked, our section cook managed

to light a fire in a hollow in a clump of trees, and soon brought us a much-desired mess of fried mutton, good bread and marmalade, and a can of tea. We rushed this as badly as the German prisoners did the bully beef earlier in the day.

It was an odd meal, as we sat by the roadside viewing a desperate artillery duel, and between sips of tea snatching up field-glasses to gaze at the bursting shells on the ridges held by the angry Germans.

CHAPTER VI.

WHAT I SAW OF THE BATTLE OF THE MARNE.

In a battle one really sees very little and knows very little of what is going on, except in the near neighbourhood. The broad perspective, the great view of a battle, cannot be seen by one pair of eyes. This can only be understood and appreciated afterwards when facts and events are gathered together and dove-tailed to form the battle story. When I was sitting by the roadside on this August afternoon, amidst the crashing and shrieking of the guns, the bursting of the shells, the furious crackling of the rifles, and the snarling notes of the machine-guns, I guessed that a battle was in progress and that we were blazing furiously at an enemy who was blazing furiously back at us. Beyond that, I did not know very much. During the night I learned a good deal more of the day's events. But the whole story was not connected up till many days afterwards. I am quite sure that the people of London knew more about the battle of the Marne from the War bulletins than I did, although I was one of the humble units present in the actual fighting.

On this sultry summer day our ambulance section

was resting by the side of the dusty road that stretched in our rear towards Paris and on our front towards a lovely green valley at the bottom of which meandered the river Marne. It wound its sinuous way from our far right to our near left. Directly before us, and on the distant side of the river, was a steep ridge, part of a low chain of uplands which rolled hazily away to the right and stopped abruptly in clear-cut lines in our front. The road beside which we sat, dipped into the valley and crossed the river on a fine stone bridge and continued through the undulating country beyond to the north. Small villages were scattered about—Mery to the right, Saccy at the bridgehead, and small clusters of houses and farms on the countryside over the river. Some squadrons of dismounted cavalrymen were standing by their horses in a meadow near the bank of the river. These horsemen had been busy earlier in the day, and had done some hard riding, cutting off stragglers from the retreating German Army Corps. Infantry were hidden from view in the depths of the valley. Batteries on our left were sending a plunging fire of shot and shell on to the ridge and dips beyond the river, and the road leading from the bridge. With a field-glass, moving dots, and what looked like waggons, could be made out on the road and the field alongside. It was on these moving dots that our guns played, and cloud-bursts of earth and dust showed that our gunners had the range beautifully.

General French passed us twice in his Limousine car.

General Smith-Dorrien passed twice—General Sir Charles Ferguson passed—all in motor-cars travelling like mad. Gallopers with messages spurred up and down the road. Guns thundered into position, unlimbered and were quickly in action. Infantry marching rapidly passed down the road into the valley where a tornado of rifle-fire was going on. One could make out the distinct note from our own rifles and the muffled one from the more distant German Mausers. Two German shells burst short of the battery on our left and uncomfortably close to us. We were in an odd position for an ambulance—in front of our own battery, which was pelting shot into the Germans and which a German battery was trying to locate. When the enemy shells fell short they fell near us. Our position, however, was a dress circle box seat as a view-point, so we stopped where we were. It was not every day that one could look on at a real live battle. Before dusk came on, an aeroplane appeared over the ridge flying towards us, and was shot at by enemy aircraft guns. The shells burst all round it, but it sailed triumphantly through them all, and to our intense relief landed safely in our lines with some valuable information.

I was much interested to see our Generals on this day dashing about in powerful automobiles. A General is always interesting at the front, be he a Brigadier-General, a General of Division, or an Army Corps General. One gets a fleeting glimpse of a "Brass Hat" in a motor-car and asks, "Who is that?" Some one with a keen eye or a nimble fancy will enlighten. "That's Haig,

1st Corps," or "Smith - Dorrien, 2nd Corps," or "Ferguson, 5th Division." "Wonder what's up?" is the next usual query, for a General moving around means that "something's up."

Smith-Dorrien is a General well worth seeing. It was "S.-D." who handled the 2nd Army Corps from Mons during those terrible hard-fought days of the retreat, and he was now commanding the 3rd and 5th Divisions on this day on the Marne, when they forced the passage and deployed on the other side.

When the action was at its hottest and every gun was busy, a car raced up from the valley in a swirling cloud of dust. The brakes were jammed hard down opposite us, the side door opened, and out stepped a well-knit, muscular, lithe figure, looking physically fit, smart, and cool in a well-made khaki uniform and red-banded cap. The face was a burnt-brick red, the moustache white, the eyes alert, wide open, and "knowing." A savage, obstinate, determined chin dominated the face. It was the chin of a strong, stubborn nature, the chin of a prize fighter. This was Smith-Dorrien, the commander of the 2nd Army Corps, and at this moment the 2nd Corps were at grips with the enemy. With a few rapid strides he had reached the battery on our left, asked some question of the battery commander, and at once clapped field-glasses to his eyes and gazed long and intently at a spot on the other side of the valley pointed out to him by the battery commander. Our party of officers, filled with curiosity, also got out field-glasses and focused in the same direction. Our shells could be seen bursting on a far ridge, and after a long stare we managed to make out what we thought were some guns, but we were not sure. A few more words to the battery commander, a careless salute, and Smith-Dorrien was back in his car, which was rapidly turned and disappeared "eyes out" down the dusty road up which it had but just come.

As the car disappeared a tremendous rifle-fire broke out all along the valley beyond the stream. It made one's pulses beat with excitement. The 2nd Army Corps was fighting hard in the valley at our feet, and Smith-Dorrien was down in the valley with his men.

When the devil's din was at its loudest, another powerful Limousine coming from the rear pulled up opposite us. "Go on, go on," shouted a voice from the inside, and the car again sped on. Inside was Field-Marshal Sir John French poring over a map held out with both hands over his knees. His car also disappeared into the valley, and we again surmised that there must be some big thing going on down below to draw thither Field-Marshals, Corps Commanders, and Divisional Generals.

An hour elapsed. All of the batteries except one had ceased fire, the cracking of our rifles was still heavy but more distant, and now two cars were seen coming slowly towards us from out the valley. In the front car were French and Smith-Dorrien. We augured that all was well, for the car was proceeding slowly, and the Field-Marshal was placidly smoking a cigar. Our augury was correct. We had forced the passage of the Marne, and were grimly in pursuit of the retreating foe.

CHAPTER VII.

THE NIGHT OF THE MARNE.

When the long day closed and darkness shrouded us all, the firing ceased completely, and the world felt strangely silent. The batteries limbered up and took the road down towards the river, and our ambulances followed the same way. The only sound heard was the crunching of the waggon wheels on the road. All else was soundless and still, a great quiet reigned over the valley which a short time before had been so tormented by the earthquake thunderings of battle.

We went down deeper and deeper into the valley, and in pitch darkness entered the quaint old village of Saccy on the Marne. Saccy is an old, world-forgotten village of narrow cobbled streets and ancient stone houses. Situated on the south side of the bridge which spans the Marne, the old village has ambled sleepily through the centuries disturbing no one by its existence, and undisturbed itself by the big events of history. During the preceding forty-eight hours the old place was suddenly engulfed in a cyclone of movement, for a German Army Corps had retreated rapidly through its streets and over its bridge,—too rapidly to stay and sack the houses in the manner so loved by the German soldiers. Their big guns had hurtled their iron messengers of death over the town from one side of the valley to the other, and sweating, panting British infantry, the finest warriors in the world, had pressed steadily along the same streets and over the bridge so lately trod by the enemy. Saccy had seen two armies pass through her, and had emerged safe and unhurt. When our ambulances entered Saccy the narrow streets were packed and congested with supply waggons, ammunition carts, guns, and marching infantry. The dull lights from shuttered windows or an open door and the occasional powerful glare from a big motor headlight lit up a scene of cursing drivers, struggling and straining horses, heavy lumbering waggons, and tired, thirsty, dusty marching men.

The headquarters of the 5th Division was established in a café on the main street, and when we passed through the staff were at dinner in the large front room opening on to the street. We saw plates of steaming potatoes, a roast leg of mutton, bottles of pickles, and many bottles of red wine. The headquarters' cook was evidently a man of resource and knew his job.

After passing through the village we turned abruptly to the right and then we were at the bridge, a splendidly built stone affair with a parapet and side walks. The bridge was fine and wide, but our crossing was a slow process, owing to the mass of waggons, buses, and equipment ahead. Some artillery and infantry had already bivouacked on the other side of the bridge, and their camp fires with dicksies of boiling stews and of coffee looked very cheerful. Some of the men were sitting or standing round the fires, smoking their ever-popular Woodbine cigarettes; others were engaged lopping off branches from the forest trees for the fire; many had taken off their puttees, boots, and socks, and were cooling their feet. They all looked very happy, and cheerfully exchanged compliments and remarks with the drivers of the waggons, who still had some miles to go before they could rest. Our ambulances were, however, about a quarter of a mile farther on, swung up a narrow cutting into a field, and here we found the headquarters of the 15th Field Ambulance, with seven ambulance waggons, supply carts, water carts, horses, tent and hospital equipment. When we joined up the unit was again complete. We had crossed the Marne behind the 15th Infantry Brigade, but our work was not yet done.

It was now eleven o'clock of a pitch black night with threatening rain. Our ambulances were packed in a semi-circle in the field near an old farmhouse. A huge log fire was blazing about 200 yards away, and round this were sitting some of the medical officers of the ambulance and two chaplains. I made my bow to my new comrades and introduced myself as the latest medical recruit to the unit, and was given a box to sit on, and a cup of hot tea, bread and marmalade. All of these officers had been through Mons and Le Cateau, and were now veterans. One who had just come in from the front with some stretchers, said that our cavalry had done splendidly during the day, and had made a very fine charge, cutting off some companies of retreating infantry. Our Lancers had ridden through a squadron of Uhlans, turned round, and galloped through them again, spearing and slaying on their two bloody passages.

We were in for a busy night, for all the stretcher parties from the various ambulances were out in the field collecting the wounded, whose arrival was expected now at any moment. An operating tent had been pitched in the field near by, and was brilliantly lit up with a huge acetylene lamp. The operating table was fixed in the centre of the tent and along each side were the instruments, basins, and dressings lying on the lids of the panniers, which made excellent side-tables. Very soon the ambulances lumbered up with the men picked up from the fields close at hand. The stretchers, each holding a wounded man, were taken out of the waggons and laid on a heap of straw near the door of the operating tent. Sixteen men were taken out and laid side by side. New stretchers were put in the waggons, which again set out to bring in more wounded. One surgeon stood on one side of the operating table, another stood opposite him, and a third surgeon was ready to assist or give an anæsthetic if necessary.

Quietly and quickly one wounded man after another was lifted on to the table, his wounds were speedily dressed, and he was again carried out and laid on the straw with a blanket below and another above him. Those with painful wounds were given hypodermics of morphia. All who were fit to take nourishment had hot soup, tea, bread and jam. Stimulants were given freely to those requiring it. The wounds were mostly from shrapnel, and only one case required an anæsthetic. He had a bad compound fracture of the thigh and was in terrible pain. We made some good splints and fixed up the limb comfortably and in good position. One poor devil had a bad abdominal wound for which we could do nothing. He was given a good dose of morphia and slept quietly and easily till five a.m., when he ceased to breathe. At one o'clock in the morning wounded were still coming in, and the surgeon on duty was relieved by myself. So with coat off, bare arms and covered with an operating apron, I did my spell of surgical duty during that night on the banks of the Marne. Our stretcher parties at last were finished, and had all come in with the report that all the wounded had been brought in. They reported that there were large numbers of British and German dead on the roadsides and in the fields. At six o'clock our large list of wounded were sent off to railhead at Coulommiers on returning-empty supply waggons and under the charge of a medical officer. The operating tent was struck and all the panniers and equipment were packed. The Field Ambulance had done its "job." It had followed its brigade into action, had collected all the wounded of that brigade, had dressed their wounds and made them comfortable during the night, and had then loaded all the wounded on waggons and sent them to railhead to join a hospital train. Having done this the ambulance was again ready to follow its brigade and do the same again. The long night was over and a new day was upon us.

This was the only occasion on the march that our Field Ambulance had to pitch an operating tent in a field. Generally a house or château was made use of as a dressing station. The tent made an excellent first-aid dressing station, but of course was unsuited for any major surgical operation, and we tried to avoid as far as possible doing much in the way of surgery. We examined every wound carefully to see that no bleeding was taking place, and all the fractures were very carefully splintered with firm wooden splints. The men suffered very little pain comparatively, and were remarkably cheerful when they had been dressed and placed on the straw. They seemed anxious to talk and review the events of the day, and they told us great tales of the Germans running away. One man said that he, with his company, was in a belt of trees lying down and watching an open space in their front. Some Uhlans, not knowing the British were so close, cantered up and halted; our men took careful aim and emptied twenty saddles with the first fusillade, and then fired on the panic-stricken, terrified horses who were careering off with the remaining Germans; when the horses fell the riders surrendered at once. The man who told me the story was slightly wounded later in the day, and had a Uhlan helmet as a souvenir of the affray near the forest.

CHAPTER VIII.

FROM THE MARNE TO THE AISNE.

AT 7 a.m. our Field Ambulance was ready to march. Breakfast was over, and we stood by awaiting orders. While waiting, some of us strolled back towards the bridge which we had crossed the previous night. It was now empty of men and vehicles. The ashes of the bivouac fires and the lopped branches of trees were all the tokens left of the passage of a German and a British Army Corps. The Marne is a deep stream with a slow current, and is a popular boating river. Two or three boating-club sheds lay pleasantly situated on the banks of the stream, bowered in foliage and trees. Up and down the river the scene was exceedingly beautiful. It was curious, when standing on the bridge, to think that in the previous forty-eight hours the tide of war had rolled over this lovely valley; that artillery had plastered the landscape with shrapnel and high explosives, and that riflemen had lined the banks where to stand exposed for one minute meant instant death; that many hundreds of men had died and many hundreds had been wounded and crippled for life. The ambulance lorries climbing out of the valley to the rear with the loads of wounded men were the aftermath of the glitter and panoply

5

of war, and of the deadly struggle in the now peaceful valley.

At eight o'clock we received our orders to follow on. So "Field Ambulance, fall in!" and away we went on the great walk to the Aisne. At this time I did not have a horse. Every ambulance medical officer is provided with a horse; but horses were scarce just then, and with three other doctors I "foot-slogged" the way. It was a beautiful morning. The night's rain had settled the dust on the roads, the sun was shining pleasantly, but drifting rain-clouds threatened a change. Major B—— and myself marched at the head of the column on foot. Behind marched the men of A Company —the stretcher-bearers and orderlies, followed by the six ambulance waggons of A Company. Then the men and the waggons of B Company, followed by the men and waggons of C Company. Water carts, kit waggons, supply and equipment carts, brought up the rear. Our *personnel* was about 250 men, and these with the waggons, carts, and horses made a fairly long column. Our road led in a snake-like way through the gradually rising uplands beyond the Marne on to the plain beyond. The countryside was typically French: clumps of forest were on our right, villages were dotted about everywhere, and there were many isolated farmhouses surrounded by belts of trees and orchards. The countryside was agricultural. The wheat and oats had been cut and newly-made stacks were standing in the stubble fields, and some of the fields still held the "stooks" of grain. About nine o'clock we came on the grim evidences of war. Our road led right through a country over which the Germans were retreating and we were pursuing. Two large motor-cars, broken down, were lying in a ditch beside the road. These were German staff cars. One had a badly burst tyre and that seemed to be all that was the matter with it. Farther on was a smashed French ambulance waggon, with a broken axle, and full of equipment and stores, abandoned by the Germans. This car had evidently been captured from the French during the German advance. Four German soldiers of the Mecklenburg Corps were lying together in a ditch. All had been killed by shrapnel wounds in chest and head. It seemed as if the four men had sat down exhausted in the ditch by the roadside and that one of our shrapnel shells had burst right over them, killing them all outright. We removed their identification discs in order that they could be sent to Germany later on. Close by was another dead German lying face downwards on the earth and with both hands extended above his head. Shrapnel had caught him full in the back of the neck. In a small clump of trees to the left of the road were two more dead Germans. One was lying on his back with his left hand over a wound in the chest. The other soldier had evidently been trying to assist him, for he had been kneeling on the right side of the wounded man when he too received a mortal hurt and fell dead across his dying comrade. His head was lying in a deep puddle of coagulated blood. The rifle of one lay some distance off, evidently violently thrown away by the first man when he received his chest wound. The rifle of the other soldier had been laid carefully against a tree within reach. The poor fellow did not reach out for it again. Two young Germans were found lying close together in a clump of vegetation. They had been sorely wounded and had crawled off the roadside into the friendly shelter of the trees. Left behind by their countrymen, grievously wounded and in dire distress, they had curled up together in the damp grass and died during the night. One had died from hæmorrhage and one from a brain injury. Another group of four soldiers had crawled into a ditch and were lying close together in their last long sleep—killed by one of our heavy shells.

A small footpath at one place ran from the side of the road towards the gate of an orchard of apple trees. Two German soldiers were lying here dead, and with their rifles alongside them. One had just reached the gate and the other was close on his heels when a burst of British shrapnel stopped their further progress. Stragglers from the retreating army, they were making for the orchard to hide when death came suddenly upon them. So the grim picture went on. The German dead dotted the roadside, the clumps of trees, and the fields on either side. Thirty Germans were found killed on a small ridge to our right. Another one was found alive, but dying. His wounds were carefully dressed and we carried him into a neighbouring cottage to die. Our artillery at the Marne did deadly execution and our shrapnel must have made of that roadside and the fields alongside a perfect hell.

Our gunners had got the range of the road and plastered it and the adjoining land with a murdering hail of lead and iron. It was curious to note how badly wounded men seemed to try to escape from the open and crawl into the shelter of a ditch or a clump of trees.

A man wounded in the field would do as a wounded stag or rabbit would,—try for cover. Some men died after crawling away a few yards. Some got some distance away into the ditches and died there, a bloody trail marking their last painful journey.

The expressions on the faces of the men were on the whole peaceful. Some had a look of wild surprise in their upward, staring eyes. Some looked as if a great fear and terror had possessed them at the last awful moment. The expression on the face of one finely built German officer, with a clean-cut intellectual face and firm jaw, was that of a sublime contempt. His eyes and nose and the curl on his lips betokened a contemptuous regard that was curious to see in a dead man.

One burly young man killed by a shell wound in the abdomen had lived some time after having received his mortal hurt, for he had plucked some straw from the wheat stack near which he lay and made a pillow of it. On this he had rested his head. His military cloak lay over him, pulled tightly round his neck. There he lay with one hand under his head and resting on his pillow of crumpled straw, and the other hand pressed on his wounded abdomen as if to give it some support. He looked like a man sleeping the peaceful sleep of utter fatigue, and when painlessly asleep his heart had ceased to beat. In his haversack there was a hard sausage and a piece of hard white bread. His water-bottle was empty and the cork had not been replaced, nor had the bottle been hooked on to his belt. Wounded, bleeding, thirsty, and exhausted, he had slowly crept off that awful field into the friendly shelter of the haystack.

The dead Germans were young sturdy men, strong-jawed and wiry. This was no canaille whom we were fighting, but a trained, determined soldiery who would fight hard and die gamely.

Our route for the remainder of this day lay through such scenes of blood and devastation. We passed abandoned ammunition trains, field guns, saddlery, field kitchens, and war equipment of all sorts. There could be no doubt about the precipitate retreat of the Germans, nor of the tenacious and pressing character of the pursuit. Large numbers of dead horses littered the roadsides and fields. Some had been wounded or killed by our fire. Some lay with outstretched necks and open mouths, dead from exhaustion, and some had evidently been shot as temporarily useless by the Germans themselves who did not wish them to remain alive for the enemy. One sorely wounded horse as we passed tried painfully to get up. We gave him the merciful dispatch with a revolver shot.

Rain fell heavily during the afternoon for about an hour and then the sky cleared again. Continuous heavy fighting was going on all day on our front and flanks, and muffled waves of artillery bursts could be heard from the far distance. The whole French and British Army was advancing in one wide semicircle, endeavouring to "roll up" two German Army Corps.

After a hard, gruelling march of twenty-two miles we reached Chiezy. It was then pitch dark and we were all exhausted, for we had been on our feet for over twenty hours, part of the time marching, and part of the time standing by waiting to go forward. When a column is marching along a road, pursuing an enemy who is every now and again making a temporary stand to get a brigade or a battalion out of a tight corner, the going is necessarily slow and there are many waits —sometimes for ten minutes, sometimes for an hour or more. The waits on the roadside are really more tiring than the steady marching. When one is "soft" and not accustomed to long walking, a day's march like this proves a torture. If such a "tenderfoot" sat down by the wayside for a few minutes, it was almost impossible to get the cramped body into the erect attitude again. Towards the end of the long, long day, and in the darkness of the night, with feet swollen and sore, brain and body numbed with fatigue, one did not march, but only stumbled and lurched along the never-ending road like a drunken man. A tired brain induces muscular fatigue, and physical exhaustion causes mental torpor. When our ambulances pulled into the stubble field at Chiezy, we had lost all interest in the war, and in everything else on this earth except a cup of tea and a long sleep.

However, certain duties had to be attended to before one turned in. The horses were looked after, the ambulances parked, and rations served out to the men. We had about twenty patients, all of them British soldiers with sore feet—men who had fallen out of the regiments on the march and had waited by the roadside for the ambulance waggons. We always ordered these poor devils to jump into the waggons and take off their boots and socks. This gave instant relief. The sores on the heels and across the instep were painted with iodine. In a few days the men were generally well and fit to rejoin their regiments.

On bivouacking this night we got all these "foot birds" to wash their feet. This was a novel experience to men who had marched from Mons without a wash or change of socks. The officers' cooks soon had coffee and stew ready, and our servants had spread straw on the ground, on which our valises were unrolled. The night was beautiful; about two miles away the guns were booming and the bright flashes of the bursting shells reminded us that war was close beside us. Without even taking off our boots we lay down on our valises and were asleep as soon as our bodies assumed the horizontal.

At four o'clock next morning we were roused by the penetrating voice of the O.C., Major X——. "Turn out, turn out!" There was no escaping that voice or the caustic remarks that would be sure to come if one did not "turn out." We all got buckets of water, and stripping in the open had a good morning bath in the buckets. It was cold, but bracing. Breakfast of coffee, bread, jam, and fried bacon. Day broke shortly afterwards and we found that we had camped on the scene of a struggle of the previous afternoon. Close by were a number of dead horses with their saddlery still on. Some newly-made graves were distinguished about 500 yards from our sleeping quarters. A German cavalry patrol had been bivouacked near a wood hard by our camping-place, and had evidently been very badly handled, judging by the signs of confusion, the litter left behind, the dead horses, the recent graves. In a small hollow I picked up a very fine German saddle and bit, and a good waterproof sheet. A bundle of letters was lying near in a small leather satchel, and on the cover of the satchel was stitched the photograph of a very pretty woman's face. Our O.C. had been educated in Germany, and being a good German scholar read the letters. They were of no military importance, and had been sent by the lady of the photograph to the owner of the satchel—evidently an officer. There were congratulations about his "promotion," and an earnest, loving message for his safe return.

Poor devil! We surmise that he must have been a

young cavalry officer in command of the patrol. His "promotion" was short-lived, for he lay under one of the new mounds of clay, and the poor lady with the charming face would have some very sad hours when she learned from the German casualty lists that "Ober Lieutenant X—— was missing." One of our men picked up here a very fine pair of new German boots. As his own were a little the worse for wear he put on the German ones, and said that they were much more comfortable than the British military boot. I believe that his observation was quite correct. Amongst other souvenirs picked up at this interesting corner were a pair of field-glasses, a revolver, a good set of razors and mirrors, an ivory-backed hair-brush—all made in Germany.

Our greatest find was yet to come. As our ambulance was getting under way one of our R.A.M.C. corporals hove in sight marching proudly at the head of eleven fully-armed German prisoners. The corporal's tale was full of interest. He was searching in the wood for more "souvenirs" when he came suddenly upon the eleven soldiers lying together in a small clearing. The corporal thought that his last hour had come. All the tales of German atrocities he had heard unfolded rapidly in his mind, and when the German non-commissioned officer got up and approached him, speaking German, which our corporal did not understand, he thought that his death-sentence was being pronounced. By signs, to the utter amazement of the corporal, he grasped the fact that the Germans wished to surrender.

He beckoned the enemy to follow him, and the eleven hungry, tired, and very dirty-looking Mecklenburghers came docilely into camp. Our O.C. approached them, took their rifles, and ordered them coffee, bully beef, and biscuits. The prisoners set to without delay, and ate as only hungry Germans can eat. Three of them had badly blistered feet, and when we marched off these were accommodated in the ambulance waggons. The remainder marched behind the waggons of A Company, under charge of the corporal who "captured" them. Later in the day we handed them over to the Norfolk Regiment, as it was clearly against the etiquette of war for a Field Ambulance to have prisoners of war. We hadn't a gun amongst us.

The capture of eleven prisoners of war by our Field Ambulance was the occasion for much joy to our men, and the corporal was a very proud man. I don't know what the Germans thought when they discovered that they had surrendered to an unarmed party. The 15th Field Ambulance is so far the only ambulance which has taken prisoners of war, and I hope that the R.A.M.C. messes at Aldershot and Netley will duly treasure the fact in the archives.

Rain fell heavily when we left Chiezy, and we were soon soaked to the skin. The roads were quagmires of greasy and sticky mud, heavy lowering clouds made everything sombre and grey, and the countryside looked mournful and cheerless. Mile after mile we trudged in the pitiless rain. I shall always remember the march from the Marne to the Aisne, for its wet and mud. Shortly after leaving Chiezy we came upon some gruesome evidences of German savagery. Near a stable built on to a farmhouse we saw a Frenchman lying dead across a manure heap. The top of his head had been blown off, and his brains were plastered over his face. The man, evidently the proprietor, had been shot the previous day by a German officer. There was an old woman at the farm, and she told us this, and that she had seen him fall. What was the reason for the brutal murder she did not know. She said that the officer and the farmer seemed to be in conversation near the stable, and the farmer appeared to be protesting at something. Suddenly the officer placed the muzzle of his revolver close to the farmer's forehead and shot him. The wound had been inflicted at close range, and we were filled with disgust at such a callous murder. About a mile farther on, we met another poor devil who had been done to death. A middle-aged man with a bald head, bare-footed, and dressed in an old pair of blue pants and a cotton shirt, was lying near a plough close to the road. His head had been battered in, probably with the butt-end of a rifle, and he had been dead for about twenty-four hours. Why the poor wretched man had been killed we did not know. The third instance of this fiendish villainy I saw later on in the day at Billy. This time it was a young man, a mere youth, and he lay face downwards at the door of a cowhouse, dead from a bullet wound in the chest. I examined the wound with some care, and would be quite prepared to swear in any court of law that the man who shot him had pressed the revolver against the dead man's chest when he pulled the trigger. This is the German way. These examples of nauseous and disgusting frightfulness amazed me. I had never before come up against such tragedies, and I felt an unholy pleasure that our big guns farther along the road were pouring shrapnel and shell amongst the living devils who did such things.

At Billy our Brigadier-General, Count Gleichen, ordered us to bivouac for the night. Major B—— and I billeted in a small cottage abutting on a very smelly cowshed. At the cottage fire we dried our soaking uniforms, and dug dry underclothing out of our valises, which we spread on the kitchen floor and lay upon. Madame of the cottage was full of the latest war news. She was *très intelligente* and very satisfied with the progress of the war. She told us that our advanced guard had entered the village only six hours behind the retreating Germans; that the Germans were in a great hurry and were too tired almost to march; that their officers were angry and cursed and struck the men who lagged behind. She also assured us that some Uhlans had ridden through, and that they were very drunk and had bottles of champagne suspended in festoons round their necks. While making some tea, and boiling eggs, she cheered us up with the assurance that the war would soon be over, for Monsieur le Curé had told her so himself, bless his heart.

The Curé opened his church and allowed our men to carry in straw and sleep there for the night. This was a godsend to our men during that night of pouring rain, and the Curé got many a rough blessing for his kind act. The villagers at Billy were much heartened at seeing the British so close on the German heels, and one old fellow—he must have been a centenarian—got very drunk on the strength of it all, and assured us that he was a veteran of the *soixante-dix* and had killed many Germans at that time. He was too drunk to remember the exact number.

During the night I was awakened by a tremendous artillery fire. The batteries beyond the village had got the range of something and were giving them hot potatoes. Madame of the cottage was very alarmed, and thought that the Germans were coming back. Her confidence in the British was not as firm as she had led us to believe the previous evening.

We were all out and ready to march at five o'clock next morning, but did not move off till seven o'clock. Rain still continued to pour down and we were all miserably muddy and damp. Whenever a big artillery duel took place heavy rain was sure to follow. This was so on the Marne and on the Aisne, and some one with a meteorological bent had made the same observations during the Peninsular War. All day long we marched or waited on the muddy, sopping *pavé* with waterproof sheets tucked round our necks and shoulders, off which the water streamed. The advance now was very slow, and we were told that our men ahead were meeting with a more organised and steady resistance. We no longer met evidences of a precipitate retreat. There were no more German dead or abandoned material by the roadsides.

At 9 p.m in the dark we entered the doleful village of Chacrise. For sixteen hours we had been on our feet and had only covered about eight or nine miles. The soft roads, ground down by our heavy waggons and guns, were in a bad state, and we walked through ankle-deep mud and slush. When we entered Chacrise we were told that all the billets had been taken up. The church, the *Mairie*, the shops, and houses were all occupied by our soldiers. It looked as if we should have to sit all night on the cobble-stones of the street, and what with the darkness, the incessant pouring rain, and the fatigue, we were all very sorry that we had come to France to fight Germans. But every cloud has its silver lining. We found an unoccupied house down a dark alley. The windows were firmly shuttered and the door securely locked. The occupants had locked up their house and bolted when the Germans were known to be about. By a little skilful burglary with a jemmy we opened a window. One of us got in and opened the front door from the inside: very soon our cook had a fire lighted and a hot supper ready. We got all our men and horses under good cover, and our night at Chacrise, which promised so badly, turned out very happily. We were all given an issue of rum this night. Rum is an oily, nauseous drink, but given certain surroundings and a certain physical state it has a most excellent flavour. On the night at Chacrise everything conspired to make the rum very palatable.

At 4 a.m. next day our never-sleepy O.C. disturbed our dreams with his "Turn out, turn out!" and out we turned. We had no choice when he was stalking round. Again we stepped out on muddy roads, and under a heavy downpour of soaking rain, and marching and stopping, reached the village of Serches on the Aisne at eleven o'clock in the morning. The rain then ceased and a glorious, welcome sun appeared. The whole countryside was bathed in a delightful warmth, and we felt glad to be alive.

We were ordered to bivouac our ambulances in a field behind the village, and were told that the German rearguard was holding up our advance most determinedly along the Aisne banks, and that the enemy artillery was in great strength.

Our march from the Marne to the Aisne was accomplished, and we now entered upon a new and different phase of the great war game. Our Brigade was in action on the Aisne banks, and we had to take up a position behind it and be prepared to receive its wounded and sick.

The Field Ambulance with a marching army takes its number from the Brigade which it serves. The 15th Field Ambulance followed the 15th Brigade; the 13th Field Ambulance, the 13th Brigade, and so on. Four regiments or battalions form a Brigade, and all the other units attached to the Brigade, such as cavalry or ammunition columns, are also medically attended by the Field Ambulance attached to their Brigade.

Our Brigade consisted of the Norfolks, Cheshires, Bedfords, and Dorsets, and the Brigadier was Major-General Count Gleichen, now a General of Division.

It was from these regiments that we received most of our casualties on the Marne, on the Aisne, and later at La Bassée, and, as the following few notes will show, we were serving with regiments who had proved themselves doughty warriors in the past.

The Norfolk Regiment was created in 1685 in the time of the Stuarts to help suppress the rebellion of Monmouth. Their badge is the figure of Britannia, well won, in 1707, for their gallant bearing at Almanza. This great regiment has done sterling service in many lands, and has as battle honours, Roleia, Corunna, Peninsula, Sevastopol, Afghanistan, and South Africa. Their nicknames are three, "The Holy Boys," "The Fighting Ninth" (they were formerly called the 9th Regiment of Foot), and the "Norfolk Howards."

The Bedfordshire Regiment, with its badge of the united red and white rose, and its battle honours with the proud names, Blenheim, Ramillies, Chitral, was a magnificent unit in France when we joined it. The regiment had been raised in the last years of James II.

in 1688, and from 1809 to 1881 was known as the 16th Regiment of Foot. The nicknames of the regiment are "The Peacemakers," "The Featherbeds," "The Bloodless Lambs." This regiment lost heavily at Missy on the Aisne, and at Ypres later on in the war it had over 650 casualties.

The Cheshires, with a united red and white rose for a badge like the Bedfords, were raised in 1689, and were in old days the 22nd Regiment of Foot. Their war record includes Martinique, Hyderabad, Scinde, and South Africa, and their nicknames are "The Two Twos," "The Red Knights," and "The Lightning Conductors"—when marching in Ireland about fifteen years ago the regiment was struck by lightning. The Cheshires have suffered terribly during this war, and at Missy we had a number of their casualties to treat, and many were buried near the old village on the Aisne.

The Dorsetshire Regiment has a proud motto, "Primus in Indis," commemorating its great services in India; and the fact that it stands first in order of precedence amongst British regiments that have seen war there. The drum-major of this regiment still carries the staff of the Nawab's herald on parade. It was captured at Plassey, where the regiment was in action under Clive.

Sir Horace Smith-Dorrien, Commander of the 5th Division, "particularly mentioned the fine fighting of the Dorsets. They suffered no less than 400 casualties. Their Commanding Officer, Major Roper, was killed;

but all day they maintained their hold on Pont Fixe." Their battle story is a great one, and includes Plassey, Albuera, Vittoria, Sevastopol, and Relief of Ladysmith. The 1st Battalion was raised in 1702. The "Green Linnets" is their nickname.

CHAPTER IX.

THE AISNE AND THE TRAGEDY OF THE SUNKEN ROAD.

On arriving at Serches on the Aisne our ambulance pulled off into a sloping grassy field, and the tired horses were taken out, fed, and rubbed down. Fires were lit and we all prepared to enjoy ourselves by resting in the glorious sun's rays, washing, shaving, and smoking a pipe in comfort. For the past few days we could not smoke in the open owing to the rain.

A tremendous artillery engagement was going on at the front. Our batteries were posted behind a long ridge not far from where we were, and every gun was in action, making the air resound with the bursting charges. It was not by any means a one-sided affair, as we were soon to know. The enemy were firing from a ridge on the other side of the river, and they had got our positions very accurately. At one o'clock a Taube flew over our position and dropped three bombs. Two fell near us with a terrible clatter, one on the road to our left down which we had come, and one about 400 yards behind us in a belt of trees. The third one actually fell in our field, and plunged itself angrily into the soft turf. Our position was obviously not a safe one for a Field Ambulance, and we got orders to retire two miles farther back. We did not move off, however, till 5 p.m.

Major B—— and I walked through the village of Serches and turned up the road leading to the right behind a steep ridge which flattened out into a plain of about one to two miles' width. This plateau fell abruptly on its northern side right on to the Aisne River. When climbing up this road, which led to the summit of the ridge, we passed numerous stretcher-bearers bringing in wounded to the 13th Field Ambulance, which was also quartered in the village. The men with slight hand or head wounds were walking, and the serious cases were on stretchers. The Germans had got the range of the ridge summit towards which our road led, and were freely plastering it with shrapnel and Black Marias.

On approaching the top of the rise we saw two of our batteries on our right, and three on our left well forward in the plateau, and busily engaged. Our guns at this date were not concealed from inquisitive Taubes by trees and foliage—that lesson had not yet been learned by the conservative Briton. German shells were bursting on the ridge in good line for our guns, but about a quarter of a mile short. Our road now took a direct turn for the far side of the plateau, and here it went through a deep cutting down to a bridge which spanned the river. On the left-hand side of the road at the cutting there was a large gravel pit or cave where road-metal was obtained. The road across the plateau was open and exposed, but from the cutting to the banks of the river it was lined with pine trees. Major B—— and myself were standing on the road at the top of the ridge trying to make out the German positions with our field-glasses. A gunner officer, seeing the red-cross brassards on our arms, hurried up and said, "You are urgently wanted in the sunken road about a mile and a half down. Two doctors have just been killed and there are a lot of badly wounded on the road." We had no dressings of any sort with us. We had come thus far out of curiosity, not expecting that it was such a "hot corner." We, however, went forward at the double along this exposed road, passing upturned waggons, dead and dying horses, khaki caps and overcoats, overturned and smashed water carts. Out of breath, we reached the cave and found how urgently necessary we were. The scene defied description. The cave was a shambles of mangled forms. Nineteen wounded men were lying in the loose sandy gravel, having just been brought in by their surviving uninjured comrades. One was on the point of death from a shrapnel wound of the brain—the bullet had passed through the orbit. There were fractured limbs, shrapnel wounds of the chest, abdomen, and head, shell wounds and concussions. We did all we possibly could with first-aid dressings. We got the uninjured men to take off their puttees, and these we used as bandages; rifles were employed as splints for the lower limbs, and bayonets for the upper limbs. One poor officer, Captain and Quartermaster M——, an old soldier with two rows of ribbons on his coat, had a badly shattered thigh and knee. He was suffering tortures, and his anguished face showed the strong efforts he made to control himself. Lieut. W——, R.A.M.C., a civil surgeon, had a smashed ankle-joint. We sent at once for ambulances and stretcher parties. These soon arrived, and the terribly wounded men were conveyed to the Field Hospital which had just been arranged at Serches.

Poor Captain M—— died that night, and was buried near a stone wall in the garden at the old farmhouse of Mont de Soissons, and the doctor had to have his leg amputated later. He was a very plucky man. Even when wounded and lying in helpless pain, he gave instructions about the other wounded men.

After the wounded were sent away I walked a few yards down the road to the place of the disaster. Here was a scene of ghastly horror. On the road lay mangled and bleeding horses, dead men lying in all sorts of convulsed attitudes, upturned waggons, smashed and splintered wood. Add to this the agonised groans of our wounded men, the shrill scream of dying horses, and that impalpable but nevertheless real feeling of standing in the face of the Creator—one can, perhaps, then feebly picture this scene of carnage, of the solemnity of death, and of the pitiless woe of this devastation. Where could one find here a trace of the glory, pomp, and magnificence of war?

The story of the incident is one not uncommon. A party of men of the West Kents were sitting by the roadside beyond the cutting, having a meal of bully beef and biscuits. As they were eating, a cavalry ambulance came up from the bridge over the Aisne. When the ambulance was abreast of the West Kents, a German battery landed a Black Maria on the ambulance, and at the same moment shrapnel burst right amongst them all. The heavy explosive and the shrapnel did terrible execution. Captain F——, R.A.M.C., was killed outright, the other doctor was badly hurt. Eight men of the West Kents met instantaneous death; eight horses were killed, and three horribly mangled and flung off the road by the violence of the explosion. On examining these dead men on the road it was noticeable that they had all received a multiplicity of wounds. One man, a burly sergeant-major, had a big hole in his head, another huge hole in his neck, a lacerated wound of the chest, and one boot and foot blown completely away. All had widely open staring eyes. The expression seemed to be one of overwhelming surprise and horror.

Poor fellows! Their moment of surprise and horror must indeed have been brief, for death is dealt out at these times with a lightning flash.

In describing events in this war one unconsciously has to turn to superlatives. "Devilish, hellish, bloody, awful, and terrible" are words that come most trippingly to the tongue. This war is superlative in all its moods and tenses. Superlative in the number of men engaged, in the extent of the battle front, in the duration of the battles, in the misery it is causing and has caused, in the awful loss of life, in the mutilating wounds caused by the shrapnel, in the number of the missing, in the atrocities, inhumanities, and blasting cruelties of the enemy, and in their wanton destruction of all that is sacred and revered.

> "Few few shall part
> Where many meet."

CHAPTER X.

MISSY ON THE AISNE.

WE left Serches at 5 p.m. and retraced our road for about two miles till we reached the ancient Château-farm of Mont de Soissons. This historic farm was our headquarters during September and till the date we left in October 1914, and it was during this eventful period that all the great stirring events "on the Aisne" took place. "On the Aisne," how much of tragedy and pathos, of great deeds, of gallant deaths, stubborn fighting, and indomitable courage are associated with those words?

On the night after our arrival at Mont de Soissons, the ambulance officers were sitting about eleven o'clock round a table in the old dining-room of the Château, when an urgent order arrived from headquarters to send doctors, stretcher-bearers, and ambulance waggons with equipment to Missy. The orders were for the ambulances to get to Missy in the dark, pick up the wounded, and at all costs to come out again in the dark. To get to Missy, which was situated on the far side of the Aisne, we would have to cross the river, and, —reading between the lines of this definite order to get in under cover of darkness and get out again in the dark,—one could see that our night ride was to be a somewhat perilous one.

Section C, the section to which I was attached, was ordered to undertake the task, and at twelve o'clock, on a pitch-dark rainy night, our section was ready to move off. We had five waggons, with the complete *personnel* of one section. Major B—— was in command, with Lieutenant I—— and myself as the other medical officers, and with us Monsignor, the Catholic chaplain attached to our field ambulance, also came as a volunteer. Monsignor was the salt of the earth, and whenever he thought that he could be of service to our wounded men he was there. There was no demand on him on this wild rainy night to leave the comfortable shelter of the farmhouse and voyage out towards the enemy lines; but he had a strong sense of duty, and behind the priest there was more than a *soupçon* of the knight-errant, who warmed at the thought of a dangerous adventure.

We were not permitted to light our waggon lamps, and in the darkness we rumbled off, anxious not to lose any time over our mission, and if possible complete it under cover of darkness.

Misfortune dogged us from the start. We had but one map; and as nobody could give us any directions, that was our only guide. We mapped out the route, Mont de Soissons to Serches—Serches to Venizel on the banks of the Aisne, where was the bridge by which we were to cross the river—Venizel to Bucy le Long, and thence to Missy. Altogether, we reckoned that we had

7 or 8 miles at least to go; but it proved to be a "long, long way to Tipperary."

After being five minutes on the march we discovered that we were on the wrong road, and it took twenty minutes to turn the waggons on the narrow, muddy *pavé* and get on again. Passing through Serches, we turned to the left and followed the road through a valley leading to the banks of the Aisne. Here again we were nearly off on a wrong road, and lost about another twenty minutes righting ourselves. The country was intersected with roads not indicated on our map. We now got on to a narrow road dipping sharply down towards a clump of trees, and here one of our waggons slipped over the embankment, and one of the horses was killed. We could not get the waggon up again, so abandoned it and pushed on with our remaining four waggons, water cart, and supply waggon. The loss of this waggon was a serious blow to us, as events will show.

As we entered the forest we were challenged by a sentry of the Cameron regiment, who passed us on. A Cameron officer met us here and told us that we were going into a bad place, as late that afternoon he had lost some men from shrapnel at the very spot where we then were. Progress was very slow for the next 500 yards, as the road was barricaded with felled trees, and trenches had been dug alongside. After negotiating this nasty corner we got on quickly to Venizel.

We reached Venizel right on the banks of the Aisne, and learned to our chagrin that the fine stone bridge had been destroyed by the German artillery that day. The engineers with superhuman energy had just about completed a pontoon bridge. We were kept waiting here for an hour. Then, one waggon at a time, we got across. The bridge was very doubtfully lit at either end by darkened lanterns, and one seemed to be very close to the swift current of the Aisne, already in flood. At the far side of the bridge our progress was again very slow for some time, as we had to meander gingerly between the trenches dug for the men who were holding the bridge-end. As we left the pontoon an optimistic engineer lieutenant, in clothes dripping with water, cheerfully called out "Good luck. Hope you get back all right." In reply we warned him that he would get pneumonia if he didn't change his clothes, and that it was foolish to take baths in the Aisne with a uniform on.

Our road lay now along a flat plain, curving to the right. The night was very dark and ominously silent. Our men were forbidden to talk or smoke cigarettes, as we were approaching the enemy lines. Reaching Bucy le Long, we inquired the way from a Scottish officer who was standing near a stone well on the village street. All his men were alert and under arms and expecting an attack at any moment. The officer, speaking with the good Doric accent, indicated our way and told us to hurry on and get under cover, as Missy was very "nasty" just then and they expected a German attack.

We realised by this time that we might get into Missy in the dark, but by no possibility could we bring the wounded out in the dark; and by the serious preparations for repelling an attack in the village street we knew that we could not get out in daylight. It looked as if we were soon to be in the thick of that most sanguinary of all forms of war—street fighting.

So on we went, and after taking another wrong turn and losing another half-hour we got on to a straight road leading direct to Missy. It was extraordinarily difficult to find one's way, as the night was dark and everything was strange and unfamiliar. There seemed to be hundreds of roads, and the greatest care had to be exercised; for a wrong turning would land us very speedily in the German lines, and none of us wished our expedition to end in an inglorious pilgrimage to Germany.

As the first doubtful streaks of dawn appeared we reached Missy.

The main street of the village was full of men of the Norfolks and Cheshires, all up and armed, and awaiting the Germans. There had been a very hot skirmish outside the village on the previous afternoon, and the Norfolks and Cheshires had lost heavily. It was the wounded from this mêlée that we were to get to. A cheery Norfolk sergeant directed us down a small lane to the right of the street, telling us that there were a lot of badly hit men somewhere at the bottom of the lane. The lane was too narrow to admit of our ambulances, so they were parked in front of a baker's shop and the horses were taken out. We hurried down the lane and found the wounded men.

Dawn was breaking and shafts of grey light and shadow were thrusting through the darkness. Then, like a clap of thunder, the German batteries opened up, and from that moment till nightfall we lived through one of the most hellish artillery duels that any mortal man could imagine. A tornado of shot and shell swept across that beautiful Aisne valley. It seemed as if all the fiends of hell were let loose. The noise was deafening, ear-splitting, the bursting of the shells, the mighty upheavals of earth where the shells struck, the falling trees, falling masonry, crashing church steeples, the rolling and bounding of stones from walls struck by these titanic masses of iron travelling at lightning speed, the concussion of the air, the screeching, whisking, and sighing of the projectiles in their flight, made an awful scene of destruction and force. Add to all this the snarling, typewriter note of the Maxims, the angry phut of the Mauser bullet as it struck a house or a gate, and the crackling roars from our Lee-Metfords—truly it was the devil's orchestra, and the devil himself was whirling the fiery baton. The steeple of the village church was struck fairly by a German shell, and with a mighty crash the stones were hurled madly on to the road down which we had but just passed, and killed one of our horses. Another shell plunged right into the old church and sent its roof in a clattering hail over the surrounding houses. A stone house at the top of our alley-way got another shell and was levelled to the ground, killing two women who were inside. The corner of the building in which we were located was struck by a passing shell and a huge hole was ripped out of the solid masonry. Shrapnel burst over the house, in the garden in front, on the doors of the house, on the roof, and down the alley. Our red cross flag and Union Jack were badly holed with shrapnel. At the kitchen door a large piece of shell fell, sending mud and gravel against the windows and into the room. A railway line ran past the foot of our garden, and stretching from this railway line to the banks of the Aisne in the distance was a wide grassy meadow on which some cows were grazing. A thicket of tall trees, surrounding a small farmhouse, was situated to the right of the meadow. This house was the headquarters of Count Gleichen, the commander of the 15th Brigade. The Germans evidently were aware of this fact, for the first shots they fired at break of day were at this house. We could plainly see one shot fall short of the house, but in a straight line for it. The second shot we thought had really got the house, but fortunately this was not so. It landed near the door, as we learned later. After this shot the headquarters galloped off as hard as they could go, and the enemy tried to reach them with shrapnel, but without success. Alongside the railway line there was a line of trenches, and every inch of that line seemed to have been covered during the day by the German fire. Their artillery practice was perfect, and at this period of the war the enemy artillery mightily outclassed ours. Our guns from the ridge on the other side of the Aisne made but a feeble reply to the terrific German bombardment.

Now for the story of our wounded at Missy. When we got down our alley at dawn on this eventful morning we found eighty-four grievously wounded men. In a little stone fowlhouse to the left of the alley, fourteen men were lying packed close together. There was no place to put one's foot in trying to walk over them. To the right of the alley a gate opened into a gravel yard of a fine two-storied stone house, a very old and solidly built building. The house formed three sides of a square; a beautiful flower garden with a rose pergola formed the fourth side. The gravel yard was in the centre. The lower story of this building, with the exception of the kitchen and an adjoining room, consisted of stables, granaries, saddlery rooms, and coachhouse. Lying on the floors of the stable, kitchen, etc., were wounded men. They had all been wounded the previous evening in an attack on the enemy concealed in a wood. The wounded in the small fowlhouse were carried, under shrapnel fire, across the alley to the big house and placed in the room adjoining the kitchen and in the saddlery room. The cooks made up a big fire and soon had hot water boiling. The three medical officers were soon rapidly at work. The first case attended to was that of a young soldier of the Norfolks who had been struck by a shell in the abdomen. His intestines were lying outside the body, and loops were inside the upper part of his trousers. Under chloroform we did what we could. He died painlessly four hours afterwards. There were many bad shell wounds of the head; one necessitating a trephining operation. One poor fellow had his tongue half blown off. The loose bit was stitched on. The compound fractures were numerous and of a very bad type, associated with much shattering of the bone. Four men died during the day, but our arrival and timely help undoubtedly saved many men. We made the poor fellows as comfortable as we could, and we were incessantly busy from the moment we entered this blood-stained place. I personally shall never forget the sight of these poor, maimed, bleeding, dying and dead men crowded together in those outhouses, with not a soul near them to help, and I am more than thankful that I was privileged to be of service and to employ my professional skill to help them in their dire hour of need. We knew that we were in a tight corner. We expected that at any moment we would be all blown to pieces; we did not know how we were to get these men back to our own lines; but we knew also that whatever happened we would stand by our helpless countrymen to the last, and if we failed to get them safely back it would not be our fault. I mentioned previously that when our ambulance got orders to go to Missy, Monsignor, the Roman Catholic chaplain, volunteered to come with us. It is difficult to attempt to write of our brave Monsignor. He was the bravest of the brave. When the three medical officers were working hard with the wounded—dressing, operating, anæsthetising—Monsignor was very busy too. He made hot soups, hot coffee, prepared stimulating drinks, set orderlies to work to see that every man who could take nourishment got it. One man injured in the mouth could swallow only with the greatest difficulty. Monsignor patiently sat by this man, and one way or another with a spoon managed to give him a pint of hot Oxo soup and a good stiff nip of brandy. This splendid prelate carried straw with his own hands and made pillows and beds for our men. He took off boots and cut off bloody coats and trousers in order to help the work of the surgeons. He rummaged in a cellar in the house and discovered a box of apples. These he cut into slices for our men. He stood by our dying men and spoke words of cheer and comfort to the poor helpless fellows. He was absolutely reckless about himself. Exposed to shrapnel and shell fire many times during the day, he was too busy attending to the wounded to think about anything else. Towards dusk, when our work eased off, we collected some pieces of shell which fell near him—as souvenirs. I looked at Monsignor many times during the day, and was struck with his expression of content and his happy smile. He was exalted and proud and happy to be where a good priest, —and what a good priest he was!—could be of such great service. I am not a Catholic, but I honour the Church that can produce such a man as Monsignor, and I very greatly honour Monsignor.

As darkness came on the hellish artillery fire quietened down and then ceased altogether. The rifle-firing continued intermittently for a little while longer and then it too ceased. We were now "up against" the last and greatest trial of all—the evacuation of our wounded. During the day some more wounded men had crawled into us, and we had now 102 men to bring back to our lines. We managed in the darkness to get two large French country carts to act as ambulances. Our four ambulance waggons were, of course, not enough, and even with the help of the country carts we could not accommodate 102 wounded men. Every man wounded in the head or arms who could walk, was told off to march with our stretcher-bearers. We packed the wounded lying-down cases into the ambulance waggons and on to the country carts. Plenty of straw had previously been placed in these latter. We were compelled to load up our waggons and carts far too heavily, but our position was a serious one; we had to get the wounded out somehow, and we had no one to help us. Our troops had retired from Missy during the day and we were left all alone in front of the Germans and quite at the mercy of their guns. The *via dolorosa* of our sorely wounded was on this night a very pitiable one. Exposed to rain, lying in the utmost discomfort, compelled to keep for hours a cramped position, they deserved our pity. The wounded men who had to march were also in a sorry plight. These poor fellows were not fit to march; weak with shock, pain, and loss of blood, they ought all to have been in bed; yet they had to march, for we could not leave them behind.

At last all was ready to start. Strict orders were given against lights and cigarettes. No talking was allowed, for the Germans were just "over the way," and they are people with "long ears."

Before setting out we buried four officers and five men in a grave by the railway, near the bottom of the garden. This mournful duty over, the ambulance moved off.

This time we anticipated no delay, as we knew the road—vain hope. The night was again very dark, and a drizzle of rain was falling. We had just emerged from the silent village on the road to Bucy le Long when the inky blackness of the night was cut through by the powerful beam of a searchlight played from the German lines. The light swept slowly up and down our column in a zig-zag wave once, and then a second time, this time more slowly still. Every detail was illuminated with the brilliant glare. The light was then fixed ominously on our front waggon, which had a big red cross painted on its canvas sides. The column kept moving slowly on, but for ten minutes that sinister, baleful light played all round the first ambulance. We all thought that our last hour had come—that after going through such a hellish day in the farmhouse at Missy we were to be finally scuppered on the muddy road. We knew that the Germans were only about 800 yards away. With strained nerves we waited, expecting them to turn a machine-gun on us. The searchlight played up and down the column once more and then was turned in another direction. My impression is that the Germans made out the red cross on the leading waggon and so let us pass. If they wished they could have destroyed us easily. We all breathed again and continued on our way. After passing through Bucy le Long, where we again saw our soldiers, we came across some returning-empty motor lorries. We placed all our marching wounded on to these and eased off the pressure in the country carts by taking off a few men. At Venizel we were held up for five hours. The pontoon bridge had given way during the day under the weight of a piece of heavy French artillery. The gun had been fished out from the bottom of the Aisne with great difficulty, but the horses were drowned. The Engineers were straining every nerve to repair the bridge. It was vitally important to hurry, as this bridge was the only artery of communication between our advanced troops and the ammunition supplies. At last we got across and reached Mont de Soissons, our ambulance headquarters, at nine in the morning. The wounded were handed over to the other medical officers. Men and officers were completely done up. We had been marching during two anxious, harassing nights, and had lived through a bad day, but—we got out our wounded.

CHAPTER XI.

ON THE AISNE AT MONT DE SOISSONS.

OUR Field Ambulance headquarters at the Château-farm of Mont de Soissons was occupied by us till October. During this time our army was fighting hard. Most of the days were rainy, and the trenches on the other side of the river suffered from this. To our right was Braisne on the river, and to our far right was Reims. To our left was Soissons—about eight miles away. We were about fifty-eight miles from Paris.

Our billet was a good one. Imagine a huge hollow square surrounded by stone buildings, and the square itself filled with an enormous manure heap. One side of the square was taken up by the two-storied old stone building containing kitchen, hall, sleeping-rooms, and offices. Stables for sheep, cows, and horses formed two sides. The fourth side was a truly beautiful and artistic one. It was formed by a wonderful old chapel, and remains of what was part of the refectory and cellars of a monastery. These buildings were in a splendid state of preservation, and were now used to hold straw and cattle fodder. The chapel had been built by the Knights Templars, and was in its day a place of renown. It is indeed a pity that such historic buildings are so neglected and forgotten. In the lofts of the dwelling-house and in a shed outside we put our sick and wounded men. In a bedroom downstairs we put the wounded officers. We were principally concerned at this time in the transportation of sick and wounded to railhead. Although we were at headquarters of an ambulance, no preparation or effort was made for any special treatment. Very few of our cases remained more than twelve to twenty-four hours. Motor lorries arrived at Mont de Soissons every morning, and on these our men piled straw and placed the men, covering all with a huge tarpaulin cover raised tent fashion on upright sticks. This method of transporting wounded was crude and brutal. There were no motor ambulances at this time. The first motor ambulance arrived after we had been ten days at Mont de Soissons. Why motor ambulances were not with us from the beginning of the war is a question which the Army Medical Department will have to answer when the war is over, and the necessary public washing-day arrives.

Several wounded men and officers died at Mont de Soissons and were buried in the garden alongside a stone wall. Wooden crosses mark each grave-head, and two of them have stone crosses erected and engraved by one of our orderlies. And the women of the house and neighbourhood attend to the graves, and place flowers on them. It is beautiful to see how reverently the French women look after our soldiers' graves. The old lady—the owner of this farm-château—has the names and dates of burial of all officers and men interred in this garden, and the relatives of these dead heroes will be able one day to visit this quiet corner of a garden in France and will see how beautifully the graves have been tended by the simple, kindly French peasant women.

Our life at this place was full of interest. In front of us were our own batteries, behind the ridge; then beyond was the river, and beyond that our advanced troops in the trenches. To our left, the French occupied Soissons. The French artillery was continually in action, pounding on every day *sans cesse* and generally also through the night, and it was excellent and well served; but our guns were silent most of the day. At eleven o'clock in the morning they would open up and leisurely plunge their shot across the valley at Fort Condé for half an hour; then remain silent till four or five in the evening, when another bombardment would commence and continue till dark.

Occasionally they seemed to wake up and become very angry, and on these occasions would bark and roar and screech for a couple of hours. The Germans never refused an artillery duel, and when our batteries seemed to wake up the Germans did too, and hurtled across their shot at a tremendous pace. The Germans at this time wasted an enormous lot of ammunition, but they nevertheless were extraordinarily formidable and effective with this arm. There was a small embankment outside our farmhouse, and this was a box seat *de luxe* every afternoon from four till half-past six o'clock. On our right, stretching on to Reims, and on our left towards Soissons, the artillery, German, French, and British, was then at its best. Sometimes the sound would be deafening all along the line, sometimes it would concentrate itself in our particular corner. Directly opposite us, on the far side of the river at Fort Condé, the Germans had a very strong artillery position. Their guns there outranged ours at first, and used on fine evenings, at the usual concert hour, to give us some splendid exhibitions. First would come one shot to the right, and then one to the left. Then four flashes of yellow flame followed by huge cascades of earth would appear to strike the same spot, and a few seconds after the dub-dub-dub-dub of the explosions would reverberate and re-echo across the hills and valleys. They would sometimes pick out one particular area of ground on our front and simply cover every yard of it with bursting shells. At other times they would plant a line of shells right across a particular place. Again they seemed sometimes to go "shell mad," and would wildly send shells to all points of the compass. In the darkness of an autumn night the bursting of the shells was a terribly magnificent sight. We could see our shells, and especially the French shells, burst over the German positions. The French artillery always excited our admiration. The great guns, the men, the rapidity of fire, the noise, and the terrible bursting charges were all wonderful. No wonder France is proud of her big guns and her splendid gunners.

About ten o'clock in the mornings we frequently were surveyed by Taubes. Many of them were most daring. They were always pursued by our men and the French; and wonderful pursuits and flights were witnessed. Two of our aeroplanes often started together after a Taube. One would fly directly for the enemy craft, and one would circle into the upper blue and try to get above it. We were told that they used to fire at one another with carbines, but we never could hear the shots or see any smoke. The Taube always made off. Sometimes a Taube would be up alone, and after hovering and circling over our gun positions would make a sudden dash to directly above a battery, drop a smoke signal, and fly away; this signal would be rapidly followed by some German shelling. The greatest spectacular effect of all was to watch the German shots from their anti-aircraft guns bursting round our aeroplanes. It was like pelting a butterfly with snowballs. We could see the burst and flash long before the sound reached us. The bursts produced white and black smoke balls, the black one appearing a little higher and later than the white. The white smoke balls unrolled themselves into a curious shape, very like a big German pipe. There was a huge bulb and a long, curling, thick stem. We stood often with "our hearts in our mouths" expecting that one of our daring flyers had been hit. Smoke-bursts would appear below, above, and round the craft, and then one shot would seem to actually hit it. But no; a minute afterwards we could make out the little machine flying higher or emerging swaggeringly from the midst. We watched our own bursts round a Taube with a different spirit, waiting eagerly for the *coup de grâce*, and having no humane thoughts for the daring pilot. One afternoon we were certain that a Taube had been struck, for one burst appeared to be right on, but when the smoke cleared away the Taube was still going merrily. Then it began to slowly descend, then ascend again, and then suddenly plane away to our right. From the last shot she really had " got it in the neck," as Tommy Atkins puts it, and the machine plunged down behind the French lines. The pilot was killed, the observer got a fractured spine, and was dragged out of the wreckage—paralysed.

On the 19th September, orders from General French were read out congratulating the British troops upon their valour and tenacity at the Marne, and commending their courage on the Aisne. We were assured that by holding on to our present positions the enemy would be forced to retire.

On one Sunday, service was conducted by Monsignor, our Catholic chaplain, for Catholic soldiers, in one of the stable lofts at the farm. The preacher and the men had to climb up a ladder placed on the outside of the building, and get into the loft through a small door. The ladder was a crazy affair, but Monsignor tested it by going up first. He was a light-weight and very active, but a burly Falstaffian sergeant looked very hesitatingly at it, and it certainly creaked and bent considerably as he slowly mounted. The loft was packed with men, and we heard afterwards that the floor was not meant for a heavy weight. We were relieved to learn that there were no casualties at the service, and that Monsignor and his flock had not gone through the floor and startled the horses underneath.

I spent one forenoon in an advanced artillery observation post, and tried to make out the German positions through a telescope. We could make out some white waggons moving on a road far off, but they were out of range. The observation officer got to his post by walking up a cutting and then crawling into a hole, and there he stood for hour after hour patiently watching the other lines, while his sergeant sat close by, well concealed, and with a telephone receiver over his head. Any observations of importance were 'phoned back to the battery. These observation posts were dangerous "spots," for they were well within the reach of enemy shells and afforded very little cover. The observation officer here was an enthusiast, and I think he was familiar with the outline of every tree and rock on the other side. It requires some practice to be really expert with a telescope. General officers occasionally came up to talk to our observer and peer at the opposite ridge. I met this artillery observation officer later on in the north of France, and this time he was a patient in hospital with a scalp wound. He had been in a house well in advance of our own advanced line, and had made a small hole in the roof through which he obtained a good view of the enemy dispositions, and directed the fire of his battery. The German is a wily man, and evidently did not like the position of this house, for he shelled it out of existence. I was glad that the major got out with nothing more than a scalp wound, for good artillerists are worth much to our army to-day. Our artillery officers seem to enjoy war more than any other branch of the service. This major told me that one day his own and a French battery got fairly on to a German battery that had done considerable damage. The Allied guns destroyed the Germans, and the French were frantically delighted, their colonel coming over and warmly embracing Major X—— and kissing him on both cheeks. We told the major that he was a certain starter for the Legion of Honour. The major was a happy man when he was standing in a hole, or peering round a piece of rock, telescope to eye, and a sergeant lying near him with a telephone receiver strapped on his head.

One afternoon on the Aisne we heard that the Norfolks, who were in the trenches on our front, were hugely delighted. They had just killed a sniper. This particular sniper had become notorious, for he was a dead shot and had hit many of the Norfolk boys. Owing to the vigilance of this particular sniper they could not get hot tea into the trenches, and several of the Norfolk "Bisleys" were keenly anxious to bag him. One day a tree was observed to rustle after a sniping shot, and at once the Norfolks sent a hail of bullets into that particular tree. This brought the man down, for winged by Norfolk bullets the arboreal

Prussian fell out of the branches like a ripe acorn, amidst the cheers of the men in the trenches.

It was said that these snipers on the Aisne belonged to the Forest Guards, who were rangers in the Imperial forests of Eastern Prussia, and were dead shots, accustomed all their lives to shoot wild pigs and wolves. They were highly unpopular amongst our men.

Sniping is quite in accordance with the rules of war, but the soldiers feel that sniping as the Germans play it is not "cricket." They naturally feel very angry with a sniper who gets up a haystack with some provisions and ammunition, and after having eaten all his food and fired off all his cartridges calmly emerges and surrenders.

Our men are extraordinarily good to wounded Germans and to prisoners, but these sniping sneaks stir their venom and ire. I saw one of these surrendered uninjured snipers at Ypres meet with savage scowls and epithets from some men of a company whose officer had been killed by him that morning.

About the last week of September I brought over some motor ambulances full of sick men to Braisne. This charming little town, situated on the Aisne and on the Marne Canal, was full of ambulances and clearing hospitals. Every house almost had a red-cross flag up, for the place was crammed with sick and wounded, and the clearing hospitals had been very busy with the big casualties. Three doctors had been killed a few days previously at Vailly when in action with their regiments, and another doctor had died the next day after having had his leg amputated for a bad shell wound. He was awarded the V.C., but did not live to enjoy that signal honour and distinction.

The clearing hospitals and ambulances were sending large numbers of sick soldiers down to the base *en route* for England—mostly cases of dysentery, lumbago, and rheumatism. Many of these men looked bad wrecks, and no wonder, when one remembers the rapid, arduous retreat from Mons and Le Cateau in the broiling summer heat, followed by the hard fighting and marching in the rain from the Marne to the Aisne, and how this was succeeded by the hardships, miseries, and discomforts in the wet sodden trenches at a time when it was impossible to give them hot cooked food and sufficient warmth. More men were wanted, and until they arrived the few had to do the work of many. The 5th Division had been promised a rest in reserve to recuperate, but not a man could be spared from the line we were so hardly holding, and so they simply had to " plug on," and, as cheerfully as they could, sing " It's a long, long way to Tipperary " ; but they did not sing much at this time.

While we were at Mont de Soissons and a week after the arrival of our first red-cross motor ambulances, we were given instructions to look out for a mysterious red-cross motor-car driven by an officer in khaki who had a beard and wore a red-cross brassard on his arm. This car seemed to be very busy and was constantly travelling up and down the roads and always at high speed—too high a speed to be challenged. Sitting at the front of the car and next the driver was a nurse, dressed in nurse's uniform, wearing a white cap, and also with a red-cross brassard on the left arm. We smelt something fishy about it all. Firstly, none of our medical officers wore beards; secondly, medical officers did not drive motor ambulances about; thirdly, there were no nurses with us. Nurses are not allowed in the fighting line. We watched for this car always, and always wondered what we would do if we did sight it, for none of us had arms, and this villain with the beard would be sure to have a loaded six-shooter near at hand. Two days after our warning the car was spotted by a sentry, who challenged, but the driver went furiously past him. He was not out of the bush though, for a barricade had been erected half-way across the road at a very sharp turn, and to get round this the car had to slow down to "dead slow." A British sentry was here, and other soldiers were standing not far away. The bearded driver was ordered to stop and get out under cover of the sentry's rifle. The guard came up and the two motorists were arrested.

The man with the beard was a German spy right through, and he was handed over to the French, who shot him at daybreak next day. They say he died very gamely.

The "nurse" who sat beside him was not shot. We were told that "she" was really a man, a dapper little German waiter who had been on the staff of a leading hotel in Paris for some years. I saw the man with the beard shortly after he was arrested. He looked quiet and scholarly and somewhat meek, but "still waters run deep."

At 4 a.m. on the 27th of September we were all "turned out" by our O.C., who had just received urgent orders to be prepared to leave Mont de Soissons as the Germans "were over the river." After standing by for two hours we got word that it was a false alarm. Something had been irritating the Germans this morning, for at daybreak they opened a furious fire on our positions. As far as we knew it wasn't the Kaiser's birthday or the anniversary of any prehistoric German victory, so we put it down to nerves. Their gunners made a dead set on a field in our front just behind the ridge along the Aisne. Hundreds of Black Marias and shrapnel were sent on to that unlucky piece of ground, and it was wonderful to see the shot-ridden earth sent up in huge volcanic bursts. The enemy thought that we had a battery there, but we hadn't one nearer than half a mile, hence our enjoyment of the spectacle.

On the afternoon of this day we heard that Mr. Winston Churchill was with us and was dining with the Scots Greys. At least that was the rumour, but we hardly believed anything we heard out here. He was reported to have said that the war would last another eighteen months. This piece of information, following on an early morning's alarm and in cold wet weather, was distinctly cheering! However, as a kind of set-off, in the late afternoon we heard that the Crown Prince had been buried again, this time in the Argonne, and that it had been authentically established that he was quite dead before having been buried. We were glad to know this, because on the other occasions when he had been buried, he had not really been quite dead.

We were at this period suffering from the effects of a dislocated postal system. I had not yet received any letters from England, and did not know if mine had reached there. We were all anxious to get the London papers to "see how we were getting on at the front." We knew what was going on around us, but knew nothing more. One medical officer returned from Braisne, told us that he had heard a great rumour there. We were all agog to hear it. After whetting our appetites he gravely told us that a Padre had informed him that, "All Europe was in the melting pot and the devil was stirring the broth." This officer was duly punished by having his rum ration cut off.

One day on the Aisne I was an interested listener to a discussion between two British officers and three French officers on national characteristics, and this led up to a review of the way that the British, French, and German charge with the bayonet.

The French charge magnificently with the bayonet, but they charge in a state of tremendous excitement. When rushing across an open space to the enemy they shout and scream with excitement, "France!" "A bas les Boches!" "En avant!" They are uplifted with the wild ecstasy of the onfall. Men fall in the mad rush never to rise again. *N'importe*—all is unnoticed, on they go, an impetuous and irresistible avalanche of steel, yelling, stabbing, slaying, overwhelming. They are superb, these Frenchmen. I have seen them charge, and know from what I saw the splendid fellows they are. In the Argonne, on the Aisne, and in Flanders, the French soldier has carried out as resolute and daring bayonet charges as ever his fathers did under Napoleon, when they stormed the bridge at Lodi, swept over the field of Marengo, and hacked their bloody path at Austerlitz.

The British charge stoically and more grimly. They do not shout. I have heard them cursing. The British line advances as a sinister cold line of steel, in a sort of jog-trot. It is a line of cool-brained gladiators, alert of eye and thoroughly bent on slaughter. Our Briton sees his foe, and smites savagely with the calculating judgment of a good Rugby forward and with the bound of a wild cat. The disciplined valour and the savage relentlessness of the British bayonet attack has been heralded in story from Malplaquet to Waterloo, from Badajos to Inkermann, and historians will chronicle the undying glory of the 7th Division at Ypres when with rifle and bayonet it held the gate to Calais.

The German, in spite of what is often said to the contrary, is a brave and determined man with the bayonet. The German discipline is undoubted. It is a part of the people. It is the fibre of the nation. Discipline, subjection to authority, has not to be taught to this people; it is absorbed into their very being. The discipline of mind and body as we understand it is not the discipline of the German, for his is an obedience to authority only,—a "go" when ordered to "go," a "come" when ordered to "come." But it is also a DIE when ordered to face certain death. Men with whom this discipline is a message may not make saints or pleasant companions, but do make sturdy foes and stubborn fighters.

They charge well, advancing with a stooping, jerky trot, uttering hoarse guttural cries and "Hurrahs." On they come, in solid masses shoulder to shoulder, hoping by the weight and speed of the dense columns to get a momentum that nothing can withstand. When in a solid compact phalanx this German charge is very dangerous and formidable, and has been able, although at a frightful cost, to brush aside and overwhelm veteran British and French troops.

But if this compact line and solid column is broken, as it so often is to-day by shrapnel, rifle, or machine-gun fire, the sense of cohesion or "shoulder to shoulder" support is lost, and the heavy column is then no match for the lightning bayonet onfall of the French infantry or the weighty heave forward of a British regiment. The German infantryman is not an "individual" fighter, but he is nevertheless a brave soldier, and knows how to meet death. All three peoples have a great respect for each other when it comes to close quarters and take no chances.

A curious feature of French bayonet charges was told me by a French officer. He said that if the daily dispatches were read carefully it would be noticed that the Germans, when they attacked the French, generally made them vacate the first trench, but that the French always counter-attacked, retook their own, and carried the charge on into the German lines. He said that the Frenchmen are very easily surprised and are only at their best when they know what they are up against and what they have to do. They also require at times to be worked up to the "fire" of the business, and that this was specially true of younger troops. The officers know this, and when their men fall back from the front trench, they get them together, tell them that they must go forward again,—that France is watching them, that the cursed German has his foot in beautiful France, that the sons of the men of Jena and Wagram must still show their metal; then drawing his sword, and with "En avant, mes enfants," the officer leads forward, followed by his cheering men, and they are at these times irresistible.

There is a story told at the front of a famous Scottish regiment whose deeds have won admiration in nearly every battle in English history, which occupied some advanced trenches. The Germans rushed them in overwhelming numbers and drove them out with the bayonet. Another regiment, composed almost entirely of little Cockneys, was called up in support, and gallantly rushing forward drove out the Germans and took many prisoners. They then told the brawny Scotchmen that they could go back to their trenches again and if they felt anxious at any time the M—— boys from London would be only too pleased to come back and comfort them. Some weeks afterwards the Kilties helped the Cockneys out of a hot corner, so the odds are now even.

Talking of bayonet charges leads up to bayonet wounds. It is a curious fact, well noted amongst surgeons at the front, that there are very few bayonet wounds to treat. Yet bayonet charges are constantly taking place, and very bloody mêlées they are.

Where are these men who have been speared by the bayonet? The majority are dead, for the bayonet when it gets home is a lethal weapon. When it pierces the chest or abdomen it, as a rule, reaches a big artery; a rapid hæmorrhage follows, and death comes speedily.

The majority of bayonet wounds are in the chest and abdomen, and ghastly terrible wounds they are. After the Bavarians and Prussians were hurled back at Ypres and La Bassée there were comparatively few bayonet wounds. Amongst the vast number of wounded men in the Clearing Hospital at Bethune I had personally to treat only one or two cases of bayonet wounds. These were, as a rule, simple flesh wounds, and were the lucky exceptions amongst the bayonet victims.

This feature about bayonet wounds was also noted by Larrey, the surgeon-in-chief to Napoleon during the great Continental wars, by M'Grigor, surgeon-in-chief to Wellington in the Peninsula, and by surgical observers at a later period during the Crimean War. A war correspondent in the Crimea wrote that a man who has been bayoneted dies in great pain, that his body and limbs are twisted and contorted by the last agonised movements preceding death. This belief is fallacious. Men who die speedily from a sudden loss of blood die easily and quietly. They go to sleep.

The German bayonet is longer, broader, and heavier than that of the Allies. The French bayonet is not a blade, but is shaped like a spear or stiletto. The British bayonet is a blade, short and light. It is not, however, the blade or the stiletto, it is the man behind that counts.

I mentioned before that our sick and wounded were housed in a loft of the farm-château of Mont de Soissons and in a shed outside. This shed or lean-to was a most uninviting place for the sick. One side was formed by a stone wall, from the top of that a roof projected, and this roof was held up by wooden pillars. There was no floor and there were no other walls. It was quite open to every wind that blew, except for the protection of the stone wall and the roof. Straw was laid on the ground of this lean-to and this straw, owing to the constant rain and the very muddy, filthy state of the roads and yards round about, got very sodden at times. New straw was then put on top of this old straw—that was all. It wasn't very much, truly. Yet badly wounded men were brought in in large numbers from the trenches and kept lying on this sodden straw for hours, and in some cases for a whole day and night. If the wounded man arrived after eleven o'clock in the morning he had to put up with a night on the straw in this lean-to. If the man was sick from one of the usual diseases prevalent at this time—lumbago, rheumatism, and sciatica—he was led up to the loft in the main house. If he had a slight wound he was also led up to this place, but if he had a compound fracture or an abdominal injury it was necessary to carry him up on a stretcher, and the stair up to the loft was so narrow that the task was an extremely difficult one, and full of pain and misery to the patient. The loft was a draughty hole and not fit to accommodate a sick mountain goat. But it was a Buckingham Palace to the Whitechapel lean-to on the stone wall outside. Yet on this dirty sodden straw I have dressed foul, septic compound fractures, have elevated a fragment of loose bone pressing on a man's brain, and have stood by men dying from gas gangrene, and from pneumonia due to exposure from lying out in the rain and cold after having been wounded. And every time I saw men lying out in that open shed I have asked, "Why have we not motor ambulances at the front?" Every morning empty lorries returning from distributing their supplies at the front called in at Mont de Soissons and took our wounded down to rail-head; and this method of transportation of the wounded was one of the horrors of war. Our wounded and sick did not arrive according to any time-table, and if they arrived at midday or in the afternoon or evening, they had, willy-nilly, to be accommodated at the château-farm, and the only accommodation we could offer was the windy, inhospitable loft or the straw-covered lean-to outside. If we had had motor ambulances all of this would have been avoided. Then the patients would not have had to be sent to our headquarters at all, but could have been carried to railhead at once. Why did we not have motor ambulances at the outset of war? God knows. Had anyone asked me five years ago what was the best way of transporting a wounded or sick man with an army in the field, I would have answered at once, "By motor ambulance, of course."

If a man is wounded in the streets of London or any other city in the civilised world he is conveyed to the nearest hospital by an ambulance motor-car. When the Army Service Corps had to arrange its transport for this war, they naturally thought of nothing else than motor traction. Yet in spite of the lessons of army manœuvres in this country, and of the dictates of reason, our Army Medical Department sent Field Ambulances to the front with the old horse-ambulance of the days of Napoleon and Wellington, and did not have a solitary motor ambulance where they were so vitally necessary. The position was so odd and incomprehensible that I wrote about it to Lord ——, who, I knew, would look at the matter from the view-point of common sense and humanity. Lord —— has a great name in the Empire, and has been one of the best and ablest of governors of one of our Dominions beyond the seas. I knew that if I wrote to him, and he chose to act as I was sure he would, something would occur. I did not, owing to army postal delays, get his answer till long after, and it was worded as follows (allowing for considerable deletions of some parts of it, and for names):

"My Dear Martin,—I received your letter in London on Wednesday night. Within half an hour of its arrival I hunted up Mr. ——. I found him in a state of great indignation because of the obstacles put in the way of —— giving the assistance they desire to the wounded at the Front. I understand, however, that sixty motor ambulances will be ready on Wednesday next, and that further ambulances will be provided later. Your letter has been read by Lord Kitchener. It arrived at an opportune moment, when the great want of motor ambulances at the Front was being realised here. I hope that even before you receive this letter the scandal which makes you so righteously indignant may have been removed and that proper arrangements are now in successful operation for the treatment of the wounded.

"Please let me hear from you from time to time how things are going, and always remember that I shall be more than pleased if I can give you the slightest assistance in getting those things done which you may think necessary.—Believe me, yours sincerely,

"——."

Shortly after this, motor ambulances appeared, and the position eased, to the infinite and lasting benefit of our wounded officers and men. I still, however, often wonder why motor ambulances were not landed in France with the other motor vehicles when our Expeditionary Army disembarked. Many lives would have been saved, and much suffering would have been avoided.

CHAPTER XII.

FIELD AMBULANCES AND MILITARY HOSPITALS.

THE military medical unit known as a Field Ambulance deserves some description.

The Field Ambulances are officially designated as Divisional Troops under the command of the Assistant Director of Medical Services. A Field Ambulance consists of three sections, known as A, B, and C sections, and each of these sections is divided into a " bearer " and a " tent " subdivision.

The *personnel* consists of a commanding officer, generally a major or a lieutenant-colonel of the Royal Army Medical Corps, who is always in one of the tent subdivisions, and of nine other medical officers and a quartermaster, generally an honorary lieutenant or captain, of the R.A.M.C. In addition there are 242 of other ranks, bearers, orderlies, cooks, Army Service Corps drivers, officers' servants, dispensers, clerks, washermen, etc. The *personnel* is fairly evenly divided amongst the three sections, so that on occasion a section of a Field Ambulance can carry on a limited but complete service. As will be seen later on at Bethune, one section of our ambulance did this, and for a time acted as a Clearing Hospital and passed thousands of wounded through its hands. B and C sections have three four-horsed ambulance waggons, and A section has four, making a total of ten waggons for the transport of wounded. The other transport of a Field Ambulance consists of six general service waggons, three medical store carts, three water carts, a cooks' cart, and an extra cart for odd jobs. The drivers and grooms have about one hundred horses to look after.

The Field Ambulance carries a complete hospital emergency equipment. Theoretically, if necessary a serious abdominal operation, a trephining operation, or an amputation could be carried out at an ambulance station by skilled surgeons surrounded by the latest and best of surgical instruments and in antiseptic surroundings. I said theoretically, but as a matter of fact such a state of affairs is not achieved, and the surgery performed at Field Ambulance stations is crude and temporary.

A Field Ambulance station is a first-aid station, and surgery is avoided as much as possible. The equipment of our Field Ambulance to-day leaves very much to be desired, and I earnestly hope that during this war the whole organisation will be thoroughly reviewed, reorganised, and remodelled, and that there will be evolved a medical unit more in consonance with the modern conceptions of good clean surgery. The Field Ambulance should receive the wounded from the Brigade which it serves, and as long as it holds these wounded it should be able to give them the very best surgical and medical help. It must send the wounded as speedily as possible to the hospitals and stations in the rear, and keep the fighting line, of which it is really a part, as clear of wounded as possible. It must conform to the demands of the military situation; for after all war is war, and the purpose of a war is to beat the enemy with sound troops and get the wounded out of the way. A Field Ambulance can do all this and must do all this, and yet it need not be too obsessed with the idea that immediately a badly wounded man is brought in he must necessarily be bundled off to the base, irrespective of the nature or magnitude of his wounds. The future of very many battlefield injuries depends on the first treatment received, and a skilled surgeon surrounded with familiar tools and appliances to ensure absolute cleanliness can be a god of mercy and confer health and power on many a stricken man. A blundering, incompetent amateur, lacking the divine essence of knowing his own imperfections and courageously taking responsibilities which are sky-high above him, can inflict a lifelong wrong and deprive a man of his power to earn his livelihood in the future. The cautious and conservative surgeon is ever the boldest when boldness means success. In every Field Ambulance in this war and in future wars, let us see to it that we have a cautious and conservative surgeon.

The medical officer is not as a rule a good horse master. From my experience (and I am speaking both from what I saw in the South African War and in this war), the medical officer is a very indifferent

A ROAD OBSTRUCTION NEAR HARFLEUR.

HARFLEUR—OUR SLEEPING QUARTERS.

TRANSPORT "CESTRIAN" IN THE BAY OF BISCAY.

THE "CESTRIAN" AT ST. NAZAIRE.

AMBULANCES AT THE MARNE.

Halt at Serches.

Gun teams at the Marne.

The way to the sunken road.

Mont de Soissons, showing the old Templars' Hall and Church.

Loading wounded at Soissons. The first motor ambulance on the Aisne.

The lean-to at Soissons. Unloading wounded.

Château of Longpont.

Village of Longpont.

On the road to Compiégne.

Compiégne, showing the broken bridge.

Ambulance crossing the Oise on a Pontoon bridge.

LOW FLAT GROUND NEAR THE CANAL—WITH A TRENCH.

TOWARDS LA BASSÉE.
Many British dead lie here.

SLIGHTLY WOUNDED AND SICK AT BETHUNE.

ECOLE JULES FERRY AT BETHUNE.

Trenches in Flanders.

Monsignor distributing medals to Belgian soldiers at the roadside.

GOING TOWARDS THE TRENCHES AT YPRES.

FRENCH SOLDIERS GOING TO THE TRENCHES.

horse master. He will do his best, as he always does in all circumstances; but it is clearly unfair to ask a doctor, who knows as much about horses as a monk does about antelopes, to take charge of a unit comprising about one hundred horses, sixteen four-horsed waggons, and seven or eight two-horsed carts, Army Service Corps drivers, and a miscellaneous lot of grooms. I have seen an amiable and competent Army Medical officer dismayed when he was compelled, owing to some duty, to get on a horse's back, and the horse seemed to know and enjoy it, for, usually a docile, mild-eyed beast, he at these times became exceedingly sportive. Yet this officer may have, owing to his rank, to assume charge later of a hundred horses and a lot of waggons. A shoemaker should stick to his last, and a doctor is only at home with his own professional work.

The remedy is to put Field Ambulances under trained officers of the Army Service Corps. They are experts in the management of convoys and transports, and could manage the field work of an ambulance to the infinite satisfaction of everybody. Leave the doctors to the purely professional work. There is enough of that to be done. Doctors are too valuable as doctors to spare them for work which A.S.C. subalterns and young captains can perform. The arranging of advanced dressing stations, the choosing of buildings as hospital sites, can be done by the A.D.M.S. of the division, and the purely workman's part of the job can be done by the A.S.C. officer and his men.

The transportation of wounded from the fighting line has been extraordinarily well carried out by the Royal Army Medical Corps and the Red Cross since our army took up its present fighting line in France and Flanders. During the great retreat the transportation was ineffective, and there is no doubt at all that many of our wounded who had to be left behind could have been rescued if we had had motor ambulance convoys as we have to-day.

On the Marne, and for the first week on the Aisne, the transport of the wounded to the base was most imperfect. Who is to blame for this is a matter that will have to be thrashed out when the piping days of peace arrive, and we have time once again to put our house in order and profit by the lessons of the war. The only means of transport previous to the arrival of the motor ambulances was by transport lorries belonging to the Army Service Corps. These waggons brought provisions and supplies to the front, and on returning empty had to call at the various ambulance stations. Straw was laid on the floors of these lorries, and the wounded were packed tightly on the straw. This method of transportation for a man suffering from pneumonia or compound fracture, a chest wound or a wound in the abdomen, was a terrible ordeal, and undoubtedly added intense suffering, misery, and discomfort to our badly stricken soldiers. Things improved directly on the advent of the comfortable, well-sprung motor ambulance. From the firing line to the horsed or motor ambulance the man is carried on a stretcher by hand, but all future transportation is by motor ambulance, train, river-barge, and steamer.

When a man is wounded at the front he is brought in by regimental bearers to the dressing station of the medical officer of the battalion. This is generally either a "dug-out" or is situated in a cottage a little way back or sometimes behind a stone wall or near a clump of trees. Here the regimental doctor simply dresses the wound, as cleanly as possible under the circumstances, stops all bleeding and applies rough splints to fractured limbs, and administers morphia if there is much pain. These regimental aid posts are dangerous places well within shell fire, and the wounded are got out of them as quickly as possible, and generally at night. They are carried on stretchers to the ambulance waggons—horse or motor—which are drawn up on some point of a road, or sometimes in a village farther back. From here the wounded man is conveyed to the headquarters of the ambulance in a village or château or church, and his wounds are again dressed, if necessary, but as little handling as possible is done, although the soldier thinks that his wounds should be frequently dressed. At the ambulance headquarters urgent operations, often of a serious character, have sometimes to be carried out, but no operation is done if the case will permit of safe transportation farther back. The next rest-house for the wounded man is the Clearing Hospital or Casualty Clearing Station, and through this pass the wounded of many ambulances. Many wounded are brought direct from the trenches to a Casualty Clearing Hospital without calling at all at the ambulance headquarters. All urgent operations are performed at the Casualty Clearing Station, and this station should be thoroughly well equipped in staff and *personnel* as well as with all the modern appurtenances so necessary for the safe performance of intricate and dangerous surgical operations.

For obvious reasons the Clearing Hospital or Casualty Clearing Station could not fulfil its destiny during the retreat of our army from Belgium to the east of Paris. If the army is retreating, the Clearing Hospital must go. It is part of the line of communications and would impede and cumber the fighting divisions as they fall back. If full of wounded at this time, it would of course be captured by the advancing enemy, as the Clearing Hospital has no transport of its own, and depends on the regular transport department of the army. There ought to be a transport attached to a Clearing Hospital and solely under the control of the commanding officer, and it would be of great advantage to have the whole Clearing Hospital under the command of an Army Service Corps officer of experience, a man accustomed to the transportation of supplies and to commanding drivers of vehicles and mechanics. To put a Clearing Hospital under the command of a doctor as is now done is as absurd as it would be to place a large civil hospital under the control of a doctor.

Our civil hospitals are governed by Boards and a Secretary who has the whole administration at his finger-ends. The medical staff do not control or govern a civil hospital. They are busy enough in their own sphere, which is a purely professional one—the treatment and cure of the sick inmates. So with the Clearing Hospitals, the Army Service Corps officer should be in charge of the hospital, and the purely professional part of the hospital, the treatment of the wounded, should be entirely and absolutely under the control of the medical staff, and completely outside the range of action of the administrative chief. The evacuation of the wounded from the Clearing Hospital to the hospital train and Base could be controlled also by the administrative lay head of the hospital, and all that the medical officers would be concerned with would be the cases suitable to evacuate and when they should be evacuated. There would at first be considerable opposition to this course by the regular Army Medical Corps, but they could not advance any cogent arguments against the devolution of administrative authority from them to the Army Service Corps.

The Royal Army Medical Corps is, or should be, a professional body of men. Anything that impairs their professional efficiency is bad. The control of Field Ambulances and Clearing Hospitals is not a professional man's *métier*, and he does not shine in this position. Too much military control or command changes the army medical officer from a doctor to a military officer, and this change is not to be desired.

In civil life the more experienced a doctor is, the bigger becomes his practice and the wider becomes his sphere of professional usefulness. In military life, experience means promotion to higher rank, and the higher the rank the less the professional work and the more the administrative work.

In war time, as witness South Africa and this present war, civil surgeons have to be called in large numbers to undertake important surgical work. The experience of medical officers of the army in peace is professionally a poor one. They are rarely called upon to perform serious surgical operations, for a man requiring an important surgical operation is no longer of use as a soldier, and is invalided out of the army. This man then necessarily comes under the civilian surgeon, who sets about to cure him, if possible, of his affliction. An urgent appendix operation, a rupture, the removal of a loose cartilage in a knee joint and varicose veins in their various manifestations—these, roughly speaking, compose the experience in surgery of the army doctor in times of peace.

In advanced and intricate surgery in the abdomen he gets no practice, and yet it is just the experience gained in this branch of surgery that is so vitally important to surgeons at the front to-day.

A surgeon at the front should be a man of ripe judgment and a good operator. He should know when to operate, and what is equally important, when not to operate. He should know whether a wounded man should be operated upon at once without exposing him to the risk of further transportation, or whether he could be transported to a Base Hospital without endangering his safety. And if the case demands immediate surgery at the front, this surgeon should be able to undertake the operation himself. Surgeons of approved judgment and skill are not hard to find, and every Base Hospital, every stationary Hospital, every Casualty Clearing Hospital, every Field Ambulance should have one officer on its staff possessing the qualities and attributes mentioned. And such a distribution is the easiest thing in the world to effect.

These men can be drawn from the civil side of the profession, as the military side, the Royal Army Medical Corps proper, cannot provide them.

There are of course able surgeons in the Royal Army Medical Corps, men who, were they in civil life, would have large consulting practices and great reputations, but these men are few and are of that surgical bent which will rise superior to its military environment, and keeping touch with modern work, will absorb all that is good and new in the methods and technique of surgery.

This lack of appreciation of the requirements of modern surgery has been evidenced in so many instances at the front with our Field Ambulance and Clearing Hospital equipment.

One day early in the war I had a number of wounded men to treat, all with dirty septic wounds. The method of sterilising our hands was inefficient and I asked for rubber gloves. Rubber gloves for the hands of the surgeon are absolutely essential when dealing with a number of septic cases. After handling septic cases he may be called upon at any moment to operate on a case requiring the strictest antisepsis or asepsis to give the wounded man a fighting chance of life. I asked a senior medical officer of the ambulance for these rubber gloves. Judge of my consternation and amazement when he said that "There were no rubber gloves in the ambulance equipment, and *he did not believe in the necessity for rubber gloves.*" When the ambulance was being equipped previous to leaving this country at the outbreak of war he could have obtained as many pairs of rubber gloves as he wished, but because he did not think them necessary, they were not obtained. He did not realise what war surgery would be like and had not been accustomed to operate on a large scale. This blunder on his part was inexcusable and serious, and the one who suffered from such a blunder was not himself but a wounded officer or man.

In a Clearing Hospital in a small town in France to which I was temporarily attached for some days, again I could not obtain rubber gloves, although I had there to operate on profoundly septic cases, on the cases of appalling gas gangrene and also on recent wounds of knee joints, of brain, and abdomen. I asked for rubber gloves and was promised them. None came. On my own initiative I wrote to a London surgical supply establishment and obtained three dozen pairs of rubber gloves by return mail.

Was this fair to our wounded ?

At another time I had a difficult bowel operation to do, and the only fine needles in stock could not be used as the finest silk available there would not go through the eyes of the needles. The examination of the silk and the needles had not been carried out when the equipment was being put together in England. At this same place I had nothing strong enough to ligature blood-vessels at the bottom of deep septic wounds, except silk. The catgut was too fine and brittle to hold a big blood-vessel, yet any surgeon will tell you that to put a silk ligature on a vessel in a foul wound is very bad surgical technique. Yet it had to be done. Again, in a dangerous operation on the knee joint I could not get any sterilised towels nor an aneurism needle nor a pair of scissors. The only scissors had been lost, and only one aneurism needle, which had also been lost, was supplied in the instrument case. The patient was an officer who had been struck by shrapnel at the back of the knee, on the shoulder, and on one foot and one hand. He bled smartly and was admitted to this Clearing Hospital with a tourniquet round his thigh to control the bleeding temporarily. I opened up the wound behind the knee and secured the large bleeding artery and veins there, and all I had to ligature these vessels with was silk. There was no stout catgut, as there ought to have been. Also I could only get two sterilised towels, and these I had to boil myself. This was in a Clearing Hospital at the front in November last year. There were no gloves. There were none of the things round one to treat shock from which the officer suffered after the operation. It made one despair. Yet all of these things should have been at hand, and could have been easily obtained by the exercise of some forethought. No wonder the wounds in so many cases were at this time sent back to England in such a foul and septic condition. It was not the military authorities who were to blame. The military chiefs did all they could to help the medical department and always have done so. The fault lay at the door of the Royal Army Medical Corps chiefs, and after the war these things will again be reviewed in order to prevent a future repetition.

My criticism is meant entirely for the good of our wounded officers and men. They deserve the best, and it is the duty of the Army Medical Department to give them of the best. It is only by pointing out defects that improvement can follow, and the only man who can point out these medical defects is a surgeon who has actually had to operate on wounded men in a Field Ambulance or in a Clearing Hospital under adverse surroundings.

It is an easy matter to arrange for a modern surgical equipment for a Field Ambulance or a Clearing Hospital. Sterilisers for instruments and towels and dressings are not cumbrous appliances and do not take up much space. The surgical instrument case at present in use by the Royal Army Medical Corps is out of date and requires a complete revision and overhaul by a surgeon who is accustomed to operate, and not by a committee of senior or retired officers of the Army Medical Staff. The younger officers of the Royal Army Medical Corps and the "professional" men amongst the seniors recognise the defects of the present system, but naturally they cannot say much. This lack of medical equipment and the "unreasonableness" of the medical department is a common subject of conversation at the front amongst civilian medical officers, and I have seen some of these men indignant beyond measure at what they have seen and met with.

The Clearing Hospital, in addition to being a "rest-house" on the *via dolorosa* of the wounded, is also a sieve. It has to sift the lightly wounded from the seriously wounded and the serious cases from the desperate cases. In this process of sifting a large collection of wounded men, it discriminates between those who are fit to be sent to the Base and those who must remain for a longer or a shorter period. Many claim that the Clearing Hospital is not a hospital *per se* but holds a purely administrative position. I feel sure that it will become more and more a hospital as time goes on, and that its present surgical and medical equipment will necessarily undergo a complete reorganisation. To-day its equipment is little more than that of a Field Ambulance. It is not equipped to deal with extensive and serious operations, and yet serious operations have been performed and will necessarily continue to be performed at the Clearing Hospital.

There is no shadow of doubt that many of the men operated upon at Bethune in the Hôpital Civil et Militaire later on in the war owe their recovery in a very large measure to the excellence of the complete sterilising equipment and cleanly surroundings. No trouble can be too great and no expense should be spared to make the surgical stations at the front up to date in all that makes for surgical cleanliness.

It is even more necessary to have the skilled surgeon at the front than at the Base, but we have any amount of skilled surgeons for both places. A skilled operating man of experience should not be attached to a regiment as regimental surgeon while a recently qualified man is deputed to blood his 'prentice hand at a major operation in a Clearing Hospital. Yet this has been done, and I know of an instance where a recently qualified man performed his first trephining operation on a soldier with a bad head injury whilst a few miles away there was an experienced operator engaged solely in first-aid work as regimental surgeon.

I was told by a senior officer of the R.A.M.C. that in the city of X—— before the war he had as assistant in his military operating room a very clever young R.A.M.C. orderly. This man was well trained in the sterilisation of instruments and dressings and in the preparation of a room for operations. When the ambulance was mobilised in this city on the outbreak of war the medical officer applied for this man, who would have been invaluable, to be appointed to the tent section of the Field Ambulance. Here the training and knowledge of this orderly would have been of great service. Instead of that, the man was appointed to look after the water waggon of an infantry regiment and was killed early in the war. Any untrained man would have done for the water cart, but a lot of training is necessary to make a good hospital room assistant.

At the Clearing Hospital the wounded man meets for the first time the Army Nurse. This is the nearest point to the firing line that our nurses are allowed to go, but I know lots of them who are extremely anxious to go into the trenches. The nurse is a welcome sight tô both officers and men, and no man nurse can adequately take the place of a trained woman. The presence of nursing sisters in a hospital is good and wholesome, and where they are the hospital work is carried on infinitely better and the patient is well looked after. R.A.M.C. orderlies do not like our nursing sisters. The sister makes the orderly work, will not allow him to smoke in the wards, makes him wash his hands and keep tidy. To the slacker, of course, these things are highly unpalatable, and there are many slackers about. Our British nursing sisters are splendid women, and work ungrudgingly and sympathetically always. It is good to see a bright-faced, white-aproned nurse amongst the wounded, and she is extraordinarily popular with her patients.

The hospital train in France is a well-run unit. The accommodation for the sick and wounded is excellent, trained nurses accompany each train, and the medical arrangements are controlled by three doctors, generally a regular army medical officer in charge and with two temporary lieutenants or civil surgeons to assist him to do the actual professional work. No surgical or medical work worth mentioning is done on hospital trains; they are simply means to an end—the end is the Base Hospital.

The Base Hospitals in France are well-run units also. There are here big medical and nursing staffs, a large number of orderlies, and any amount of equipment. I was for some time Surgical Specialist at No. 6 General Hospital at Rouen, and this hospital was splendidly administered by the commanding officer, Lieutenant-Colonel ——. In the Base Hospitals there are good operating rooms, and in fact every modern appliance that one could desire. It is a pity that the same care in administration and equipment had not been carried farther up and nearer our soldiers at the front.

CHAPTER XIII.

GOOD-BYE TO THE AISNE.

EARLY in October, and at night, the Ambulance again took the road—we turned our back on the Aisne and with the 2nd Army Corps began the famous move across the French lines of communication to the Belgian frontier and into Flanders. This change of position will be written up in the future as one of the most masterly episodes of the war. It was a formidable task to move the British Army and its supplies across the French lines and bring them into an entirely new position on the front. It had to be carried out with the utmost secrecy. None of us knew where we were going. Each day the secret orders were issued and the various brigades and columns carried out the indicated programme, while the French took up our positions and trenches as we retired from them. This was done also with great secrecy. I can imagine the perturbation of the Saxons and Wurtemburgers on our front on seeing French *képis* and uniforms where for weeks they had seen the khaki. The 2nd Corps moved off first. The 1st Corps left a week later.

On the first night we marched through Nampteuil and reached Droszy about midnight. It was a beautiful starlight night with a biting frost. We billeted in a spacious château, with plenty of cover for the ambulance waggons and with stables for the horses. The men slept in stable lofts and the officers on the floor of the marble hall. The hall was a beautiful room, containing some valuable old furniture. The walls were covered with relics of the chase of the days of Louis XIV., and old hunting horns, knives, and boar spears. Part of the château was modern, and part consisting of a wonderful old tower, loopholed for arrows, was evidently all that was left of the keep of a strong feudal castle. The proprietor was an old rear-admiral of the French Navy and he received us with the greatest courtesy; the Norfolks arrived an hour after us and quartered in a big house and yard close by. Our brigadier, Count Gleichen, arrived early in the morning and slept in our château.

A Taube was seen approaching in the morning and every one was ordered to get under cover or stand stock-still. This Taube was evidently trying to find out the reason for the absence of British in the old trenches and the presence of the French in their place. We surmised correctly that the Teutonic curiosity was considerably aroused. A few hours afterwards another Taube appeared—or it may have been our first visitor—and flying very fast, for a French airman was in hot pursuit. Both soon disappeared into the upper blue, but we laid our odds on the Frenchman.

At 6.30 that night we again got under way and had a magnificent night march to Longpont, arriving there at

10.30 p.m. Longpont is a wonderful old place. The Château Longpont dates back to very early times and contains some marvellous old tapestry. It is the home of the Comte and Comtesse M——, and they were in residence at this time and entertained as their guests on this day General Sir Charles Ferguson and his staff. Sir Charles was the Commander of the 5th Division of the 2nd Army Corps. The Comte and Comtesse had as guests, some weeks previously, General von Kluck, Commander of the right wing of the German Army, and had some interesting anecdotes to tell of this hard-fighting General and his staff.

Abutting on the château were the famous ruins of the abbey of Longpont. The remains of the old abbey are so historic that they are known in France as "Les Ruines." It was built by the Cistercian monks in the twelfth century, and in the adjoining priory over three hundred monks were accommodated in the days when the Church was omnipotent in France. During the Reign of Terror the beautiful old abbey was destroyed by the revolutionaries, but the massive character of the pillars and walls proved too much even for these iconoclasts, and stand to-day, clothed in ivy and moss, the monuments of a glorious past. The venerable and stately majesty of these ruins, where every stone seemed to speak of the grandeur of other days, impressed the imagination of all who gazed upon them.

The day following our arrival at Longpont was a Sunday. Divine service was conducted at 10 a.m.

round the old broken altar by our Church of England chaplain, and Sir Charles Ferguson, the Divisional General, read the lessons. Monsignor conducted the Catholic service at 11.30. Both services were largely attended by our own men and by French soldiers occupying the village. In imagination one could see the princely abbots and the cowled monks who, during a period of six hundred years, had chanted their litanies and passed in procession inside the beautiful abbey, gazing wonderingly at the simple military services held round the tumbled masonry of the ancient altar.

After the services we spent the day wandering through the old-fashioned village of Longpont, examining its ancient gateways adorned with the crests of the kings of France, or strolling through the fine woods bordering the lake. Heavy artillery fire from the French batteries could be heard all the day. We were now right behind the French lines.

I cannot pass from Longpont without describing our sleeping quarters on the night of our arrival. The officers of the ambulance had to sleep on the straw of an old stone stable. The stable looked comfortable and inviting, and it was not till we had crawled into our valises that the "fun" commenced. We had just lain down and blown out the candles when we felt curious obscure movements under our valises. Then a rustling of straw and a scampering of some objects over our beds. One doctor at once yelled out, "Good Lord, the place is full of rats." He turned on his electric torch and immediately there was a wild scurry and stampede to cover of hundreds of rats. The torch was turned off, and after a little while the scampering and squeaking started again. The rats were either enjoying a game or were upset by our occupation of their stable. At one end of the stable was a feeding trough, and sitting in a row on the edge of the trough were innumerable rats. Conspicuous amongst them was one enormous fellow, about the size of a cat—some one said he was as big as a calf—with huge grey moustaches and very knowing eyes. This was undoubtedly the leader. We christened him Von Hindenberg. Somebody threw a bottle at him, but the cunning old rascal dodged it by making a tremendous leap into the middle of the stable and disappeared. One young doctor then said that he would rather sleep out in the open than amongst the rats, and he carried his valise outside. The rest of us decided to stop where we were, but we all pulled our blankets well over our heads. Our childhood horror of rats still remained, and we were just a little bit afraid of them—especially of Von Hindenberg.

From Longpont we had a hard gruelling march of fifteen to eighteen miles through the night, and arrived at Lieux Ristaures at 6 a.m. We were stopped a long time on the road at the little village of Corcy by hundreds of motor vans, waggons, and buses containing French troops. We realised on this night what "crossing a line of communication" actually means. The French were hurrying up heavy reinforcements to strengthen a part of their front which at that moment was withstanding a most resolute German attack, our Brigade was moving as quickly as possible to another point of the front. The roads of the two armies crossed at Corcy, and of course one had to wait till the way was clear. It all looked very confusing and chaotic, but it was really very cleverly managed. Our road at first led through a forest, and anyone who knows the forests of France knows the beauty and charm of the tall trees. Little could be seen, however; high overhead one could make out a few stars, but the track itself was in Cimmerian darkness. About 2 a.m. we reached Villars Cotterets and marched through the old cobbled streets without a pause. This old town looked interesting, and one would have liked to have explored the birthplace of Dumas. After Villars Cotterets our road lay through more open country and a grey dawn made things clearer. We were all dog-tired with the long march and the constant halts; marching at night was more monotonous and fatiguing than day marching.

On the way from Villars Cotterets to our next bivouac, Lieux Ristaures, at night time, when we were all feeling very done up, a most surprising rumour reached us. Far ahead on the long column we suddenly heard distant cheering which grew in intensity as it travelled quickly down to us preceded by a message shouted from one to another, "The Kaiser is dead. Killed yesterday morning. Pass it on." When the message reached us we laughed, and did not pass it on. Cries came out of the darkness in front, "Pass the message on. It's official. The Kaiser's dead." So we passed it on, and the cheering travelled back across country to the marching men far behind. It cheered the men up wonderfully; they were delighted. It of course turned out to be a fake, cleverly engineered by some wags at the head of the column. Of rumours there was no end. The Crown Prince had been buried in Flanders, in the Argonne, at Soissons. But he always got out of his grave. We buried Von Kluck, Hindenburg, and Bulow, and each burial was related with a wealth of detail that left nothing to the imagination. The most accepted rumour of all, and one which is still believed by many, was the harrowing story of the Prince with the velvet mask. This story had a distinctly Dumas flavour, and it had a great vogue. It was related to me first on the Aisne by a doctor in a Scottish regiment, who had had it from the Colonel, who had received it from somebody higher up. I, of course, passed it on lower down the social scale, and our Division knew it that afternoon. The Crown Prince at this time was said to be living in a richly furnished cave opposite Reims. On dull days he would sit on a chair outside and order the shelling of Reims Cathedral, while he gazed through a powerful glass at the falling masonry. One day the Prussian Nero was missing from his cave, and the story then shifts to Strasburg, whither in the dead of night a wounded officer of apparently august rank was conveyed in a motor-car. Two powerful Limousines accompanied this car, one before and one behind, and these were full of highly placed army officers. A special train with steam up was awaiting the arrival of the cars, and as the wounded officer was carried across the platform on a stretcher, closely surrounded by Generals, it was noticed that a velvet mask covered his face. The mask fell off as the body was lifted into the train and the Crown Prince's face was exposed to view. I believe that this story was afterwards circulated in the French press. We certainly did not hear of His Imperial Highness for many months afterwards.

Another rumour circumstantially related by a field chaplain and duly passed on with the *imprimatur* of the Church, was that Prince Albrecht of Prussia, son of the War Lord himself, had been wounded and taken prisoner into Antwerp by the Belgians. He was operated upon by Belgian surgeons in the presence of two German medical officers, and a bullet was extracted from his spine. The bullet was a Mauser—a German one. The Prince died and his body was handed back to the Germans.

On the way to our next bivouac we also heard that Arras was being bombarded by the Germans and that they were investing Antwerp. We had quite a lot of war news to discuss for the remainder of our road, and until we pulled our waggons under the trees round an old mill at Lieux Ristaures. The men were billeted in outhouses and wood sheds belonging to the mill, and the officers were cordially welcomed by the hospitable miller and his kind-hearted womenfolk. They prepared coffee, bread and butter, and eggs for us, and we had the use of two bedrooms and a small office. A rapid mill race ran through the garden and under the kitchen floor of the house to the orchard beyond. When the miller's wife wanted fresh water, all she had to do was to lift up a trap on the kitchen floor and dip the bucket into the tumbling water below. Lieux Ristaures has a fine old ruined church all to itself, but it is disfigured by some modern attempts to restore it to its ancient grandeur, and these attempts have spoiled completely the beauty of the ruins. At Lieux I received my first mail since leaving England. It was now October, and I had left England in August. This will give an idea of the marvellous work of our Army Post Office, but as no department has received such abuse as this one, I will spare its feelings and say no more.

A fine contingent of French cavalry passed by on this day. The men and horses looked splendid. The brass helmets, plumes, and cuirasses caught the sun's rays, and we described the passing as a "gorgeous cavalcade." The helmets and cuirasses, however, seem to belong to old-world armies, and look stagey amongst the simpler uniforms of this age.

We stopped two nights at the quaint old farm of Lieux with its rushing mill race, and at three o'clock on the second day marched to Bethisy St. Martin, where we had an excellent tea at a cosy house in the town —butter, eggs, bread, cold beef, and pickles. We sat round a table with a tablecloth! our first since August. The good woman who prepared the meal made us very welcome. We slept on the floor of the

Mairie in the centre of the town till 5 a.m., when we again took the road to Santines and Verberie, passing near Senlis. Verberie showed many evidences of the Prussian sign manual—shelled houses and smashed walls. We reached the river Oise at 10 a.m. and crossed by a pontoon bridge, as the fine old stone bridge had been blown up; marched through Rivecourt and bivouacked for three hours by the wayside. It was a glorious morning, the going was good, and everybody was cheerful and looked very hard and fit. At Halte de Meux, where was a railway siding with troop trains, we received orders to embark on one of the trains for a destination unknown.

The train by which we were to travel had to carry the Norfolk Regiment also. When the Norfolks were all on board we found that there was not room enough left for the Field Ambulance, with its ambulance waggons, supply waggons, horses, and men. C section, with its waggons and equipment, had to be left behind, and get on as best it could by some other train; so we of C section took the road to Compiègne. We reached this charming and historic city in the dark, and found that there was no train for us. We crossed the Oise again on a bridge of moored barges, as the magnificent stone bridge spanning the Oise here was in ruins, destroyed by the French during the German advance. The night was desperately cold; we slept, or tried to sleep, on the boulevard alongside the river bank, but had to get up and march about to keep up the circulation. The men lit a fire under the trees of the boulevard and sat round it all night. There was no reason really why we should have slept out on the open boulevard, for there was a large, half-empty infantry barracks about 20 yards away and the French offered us the use of it for the night. Our commanding officer, however, decided otherwise, and consequently we passed a most miserable night.

Compiègne, situated on the Oise, is one of the most charming and fascinating cities in France. In the palace, Napoleon Bonaparte and the Empress Marie Louise, Louis Philippe, and Napoleon III. frequently resided. The tower where Joan of Arc was imprisoned, the sixteenth-century Hôtel de Ville with its belfry tower, and the old church of St. Jacques well repay a visit. The city appeared on the surface to be leading a normal life except for the large number of French soldiers and the many Red Cross Hospitals. Compiègne was at this time a favourite afternoon call for the Taubes, and they frequently dropped bombs, meant no doubt for the old palace. Old historic châteaux, cathedrals, and churches have a strange fascination for German artillerists and bomb-droppers.

I must now relate an episode of some interest that occurred on the march up to Compiègne — nothing less than seeing General Joffre, the Commander-in-Chief of the Allied Armies. I had dropped behind from my ambulance, and had given my horse to my groom to lead behind my section on the march. A marching regiment was coming up behind us, and as I knew the doctor I waited till the regiment came up, and then joined in and walked alongside my medical friend. A large château was situated on the side of the road some distance on, and as we came up we saw a large group of French officers standing at the old gateway. A whisper travelled rapidly down the line that this was the French Headquarters Staff and that Joffre himself was there. At once the subalterns "tightened up" the marching men, heads were lifted, shoulders squared, the step became smarter and rhythmic. Low muttered commands snapped out: "Smartly there," "By your right," "Keep your distance, men." As we came abreast of the group at the gateway, the sharp, clear command rang out from each platoon officer, "Eyes right!" the officers saluted smartly, and with a parade swing the fine regiment marched past. I gazed long and interestedly at the officer at the gateway who took our salute. He was easily distinguishable as Joffre, for he was exactly like the pictures seen of him in every shop window in France, or rather the pictures were faithful representations of Joffre. When I got past, I stepped out of the company I was marching with on to the far side of the road, and while the remainder of the regiment was still passing by I had a good long look at the man who means so much to France, and in whom France is so sublimely confident. He was dressed in a well-fitting but easy blue tunic, with stars on the sleeves near the cuff indicating his rank of General, and with a gold band on the shoulders, the familiar red French trousers, and black polished cavalry jack-boots. On his head he had a gold-braided *képi*.

Joffre is of middle height, strong and sturdily made, broad-shouldered and with a figure stout and heavy. His face is full, genial, and attractive, browned like the faces of men who have lived and worked in the tropics, and with a white moustache which gave a somewhat benevolent air. He was evidently interested in the march past of our regiment, for he walked three or four paces forward from his staff and towards us, and seemed to take in all the details of men and equipment as his eye scanned up and down. His salute was given with the careful exactness and ceremony always bestowed by the French upon this act, which the British officer goes through so casually.

Joffre did not look the dazzling military leader of romance, but he looked very business-like. Here was not the lean figure and the hawk nose of a Wellington, the glittering swagger of a Murat, or the inscrutable pose of the little Grey Man of Destiny. Yet this broad, homely, comfortable, and democratic figure standing by the roadside and carefully observing us, is the most powerful man in France to-day—the man against whom no political criticism is levelled, the idol of the soldiers, and in whom the people of France have such a simple faith. He is called "Our Joffre," and the possessive phrase indicates the pride the people and army feel in him. The French will tell the following story, which has gone the rounds, with great gusto. After a big battle in Poland, Von Hindenberg's Chief of Staff contracted a "political illness" and was sent to Berlin to recover his health.

The Kaiser wired to Hindenberg, "Whom do you nominate for your new Chief of Staff?" The reply came back, "Would like Joffre."

French officers at the front will tell you that Joffre is an Aristides the Just; that he ordered the shooting of four French Generals early in the war because they were traitors to France, and that he has "retired" all the old Generals who are slow to think and too fond of cocktails to be good campaigners; that he speedily rewards ability and initiative by promotions on the field, and is merciless on an officer—no matter of what rank—who shows incompetence.

Joffre was met early in the War of the Trenches by an old friend, who greeted him with, "Well, how are things going?" The General's eyes twinkled humorously as he replied, "Laissez-moi faire, je les grignotte" ("Leave me alone, I am nibbling them"). A French surgeon who knows Joffre, told me that he is a good sleeper, and that during the worst days he never missed one night's sleep. It was Shakespeare's Cæsar who said, I think, to Mark Antony:

> "Let me have men about me that are fat,
> Sleek-headed men and such as sleep o' nights."

Joffre has never interested himself in politics, and he is one of the few great Frenchmen who have avoided the glamour of the political stage on which so many ephemeral reputations have been made and so many good ones blasted. Joffre, like most men who "do" things, is a silent man. I am glad that I have seen "Joffre *le taciturne*," and been privileged to salute him.

Joffre and French are both over sixty years of age. Pau, the one-armed French General, known as the "Thruster," is a veteran of the War of 1870. Gallieni, the "rock of Paris," the General destined to hold Paris when Von Kluck was bearing so hastily down on the capital, is an old man. Von Hindenberg, the pride of Germany, is sixty-seven. Von Kluck, the Commander of the right wing of the German Army, who so furiously hacked his way almost to the gates of Paris, and was rolled back in a crushing defeat, is over seventy years of age. Napoleon and Wellington were forty-six at Waterloo. Nelson died at forty-seven. Ney was thirty-five when he was shot. Von Roon, the German Minister of War in the Franco-Prussian War, was sixty-seven when the campaign began. Bismarck was then about fifty-five, and Von Moltke was an old man—a septuagenarian. Are we too old at forty? No. I knew a chaplain at the front who was fifty-eight years of age. In times of peace he took very little physical exercise; he was a student, a scholar, and an author. I have seen this chaplain march mile after mile in rain and mud, and under a broiling sun on dusty roads, and he was then fitter than he ever had been before, and could eat bully beef and hard biscuits like the hungriest youngster. He had the face and eyes and voice of a young man, and he laughed like a merry boy.

We left Compiègne at 3 p.m.; our horses and waggons were entrained and officers and men got into an old and evil-looking "100th" class carriage and again set off for a destination unknown. No one seemed to know where we were off to, but the entraining and route were really well carried out by the staff of the railway. At Amiens we received orders to get off at Abbeville, and after a tiring journey we reached the mouth of the Somme at 2 a.m. The waggons and horses were quickly taken out, and in the dark we trekked through Abbeville across open country to Gapennes, nine miles away. Here we met the 13th Field Ambulance, temporarily quartered in a most luxurious château. Our little party was dead beat for want of sleep, and some of us lay down on the floor of the village schoolhouse and slept heavily for three hours. The school was not "in" that day, otherwise I am sure the children would have been highly entertained to see three weary doctors in khaki soundly slumbering on the floor.

Still sleepy, we again had to take the road and tramp the weary miles. A large number of French ambulances passed us going back to Abbeville, and we heard that there had been some very hard fighting on the French left wing.

The 13th British Infantry Brigade caught up with us, and we pulled aside to let them pass. The officers told us that they were in a hurry—that the French had moved up a lot of troops to the south of Lille and that the whole British Army was to form up on the left of the French, and that terrific fighting was going on round Lille and Arras, and French and German cavalry screens had met farther west.

At 5 p.m. we found the headquarters of our ambulance located in a pig-sty of a farmhouse and were told that it was to move off shortly and march through the night. All the romance of night marching had gone for us, and we wanted to sleep. We were tired of walking, tired of everything, tired of the war, and vaguely wondered why we had been so foolish as to leave England.

So at nine o'clock on the same evening off we marched again into the outer darkness of a depressing, gloomy night, and we were on our feet through the whole of it. Most of the time we were standing by the roadside waiting for the congestion of the long columns in front to ease off. Sometimes we would sit in a ditch by the roadside and go off to sleep, only to be wakened a minute after by the cry, "Forward!"

About 6 a.m. we reached Croisette. The name sounds attractive, but it really was a mean-looking farmhouse at a cross-road; however, we got a very good breakfast of coffee, bread and fresh butter, and eggs. The farmer's wife was anxious to know how the war was going on. She rarely got news, but heard lots of rumours. Everybody appeared to be hearing rumours as well as the British Army. We told her that we had killed thousands of Germans and were on the way to slaughter those that were still left; and as this appealed to the patriotic instincts of the farm lady, she was very satisfied with our latest war bulletin.

In three nights and three days I had had only three hours' sleep, and had got to a stage when I marched, rode, and ate my food in a sort of subconscious state of reflex animation. In the late afternoon we rumbled into Thielyce, and tried fruitlessly to find some billets for our officers and men. The place was full of small cottages, and the cottagers eagerly offered each to take in one or two men; but we could not allow this, as in the event of sudden orders through the night we might not be able to get all our men together. We always lived in one large party or habitation like gipsies. One old woman of the village was extremely anxious to have some khaki soldiers stop at her house. She was curious to observe the English at close quarters, as she had never seen one before and had heard that they were such terrible fighting men. Our looks belied our reputation; we looked harmless, very dirty and dusty, but very tame.

The ambulance was parked in a field off the village street and inside a delightful clump of trees. Too tired to eat, I lay down as I was, armed cap-à-pie, at the foot of a tall umbrageous tree and slept a dreamless sleep.

At five o'clock next morning the sharp call of our O.C., "Field Ambulance, turn out!" aroused me again to a world of marching men and war; but I was my own man again and optimistic, and no longer wondered why I had left England.

We had a picnic breakfast sitting on the grass in the field, and at seven o'clock received orders to move off: we were to follow the 13th and 14th Brigades into Bethune and on to La Bassée, and be prepared for big casualties, as a stern battle was expected and the two brigades would probably be in action before midday. There was a feeling of expectancy in the air that morning. All the rumours about a big battle and all our quick movements and marchings by night seemed to presage a clash at arms. We hoped for old England's sake that we would do well; our pulses were stirred and we were all very much alive.

We moved off smartly down a fine old tree-lined road towards the sound of heavy guns which had been in action from daybreak. On our way we passed thousands of hurrying refugees going towards St. Pol. Without stopping, our ambulances growled their way through the ancient cobble-stoned town on to the big high road leading to Bethune. Here again we met thousands of refugees, nearly all young men of military age. We were curious to know why these men were not in the French Army, and a French officer told us that they belonged to Lille and the surrounding districts, and had been ordered out by the French authorities to report at military dépôts farther south for training and active service. These "mobilisables" would have been good captures for the Germans and a considerable loss to the French Army. Amongst them I counted twenty-seven priests in black caps and cassocks; they, too, were on their way to shoulder a French rifle. One young man I noticed carrying a white rabbit in a bird-cage in one hand and a bundle of clothes and boots in the other; he was saving his rabbit from a German pie. Another fellow was walking along the road in carpet slippers and with a pair of heavy boots suspended round his neck.

The poor refugees looked tired, disappointed, and depressed, and no wonder. It is hard suddenly to have to leave your home, your friends, your wife and children, and to go away with a gnawing fear that they will be in the power of an arrogant and brutal enemy who knows no mercy. We pitied them all.

After all, there was no battle that day. We halted on the way some time, and then were rapidly marched forward towards Bethune. We were now passing through coal-mining towns and villages, and they recalled very much the villages and houses round coal areas of Scotland like Falkirk. The type of coal-miner and the coal-miner's cottage are very much the same all over the world. These people did not seem very curious or interested in our passage through their villages or towns — simply gave us a glance at passing.

That night we bivouacked in a château near Bethune and on the main road. We could not get any farther forward, for the road in front was blocked up by big guns and little guns, ammunition columns, engineer battalions, and infantry. We saw a number of waggons loaded up with big pontoon boats, and speculated that we must be near water. So we were. We were near the famous canal, but the boats were intended for farther west.

After tea in the kitchen of the big château, some of us got on our horses and rode into the city of Bethune, now full of troops, and the bustle of warlike preparations. There were all nationalities in the streets of Bethune that night. Arabs in flowing robes were on horseback in the square, looking strangely out of place in this old western city. Spahis, French Grenadiers, French gunners, Alpine Chasseurs in round cloth caps, Belgian, French, and British officers, and, of course, Mr. Thomas Atkins, quite at home, smoking a Woodbine cigarette and being petted and openly admired by the women and the girls. We heard here that Antwerp had fallen, and thought the news very serious. It was quite unexpected, as we had not known that it had been strongly besieged.

At five o'clock next morning we were on the road in a dense fog, and after going forward about half a mile were told to bivouac in a field near the road till some ammunition columns and guns got past us. This we did, but Monsignor wandered off alone farther down the road. We missed him for a long time, and when he did turn up he told us that he had been arrested as a spy by the French. Two or three French sentries with fixed bayonets surrounded him, and I don't know what arguments Monsignor used to convince them that he was an Englishman. But he came back smiling, and was evidently much tickled over the whole affair. He was the only officer in the British Army, and in fact the only member of the Expeditionary Force, who was not in khaki uniform, and it is no wonder that the French thought it odd that he should be strolling about "on his own," looking at British guns and equipment. We were all delighted, of course, at Monsignor's arrest, and regretted that we had not been there with our cameras. We were quite determined, if he were again arrested, to disown all knowledge of him, just to see what the French would do next.

After some hours' wait in the field we pushed on again through Bethune towards the canal. This canal was to us then simply a canal and nothing more, but along this belt of slowly flowing water was to be waged very soon one of the most terrific and sanguinary struggles recorded in history.

As we approached the canal the Norfolk Regiment came up, and we drew to the side of the road to give them the right of way. I sat on a heap of stones by the roadside and watched this fine regiment marching smartly past, and I remember thinking curiously that probably that same day, perhaps within a few hours, many of these fine fellows would have fallen and many would be maimed.

It is an impressive thing to see a regiment going into action. The Norfolks knew that they would very soon be in the thick of things, as they were marching on the sound of the heavy guns, but they looked perfectly cheerful and unconcerned. That night several of them passed under my hands on the operating table, and many more were lying very still on the wet earth not far away.

The King's Own Scottish Borderers passed us earlier in the morning, and with them was Dr. D—— as regimental surgeon. D—— was one of the first medical officers over the Aisne, and he put through some splendid service for the wounded under a heavy fire, and was mentioned in dispatches. Four days afterwards poor

D—— and his stretcher-bearers were captured and sent as prisoners to Germany.

At 11 a.m. we crossed the narrow bridge spanning the now famous canal leading up towards La Bâssée, and installed our ambulance headquarters in the Château Gorre on the road to Festubert. The château had up till that day been the headquarters of a French cavalry general, and it was a most palatially fitted-up place.

Our long journey was over. We had left the Aisne and taken up a new position near La Bassée in the north of France. We were now in a countryside destined soon to become the theatre of an intense and sanguinary struggle. It was here that our men withstood the shock of the most determined and relentless head-on attacks of the enemy. This was one of the roads to Calais, and we held the gate.

CHAPTER XIV.

THE LA BASSÉE ROAD AT CHÂTEAU GORRE.

As the fighting is still going on round this district any description of military positions or dispositions would be quite out of place.

Our headquarters at Château Gorre was a beautiful two-storied stone building, quite modern, and well arranged in every way with spacious lofty halls, dining-rooms, lounges, bedrooms, and bathrooms.

When we took up our quarters here we knew that we would soon be busy with wounded, and the central hall of the château was at once prepared for their reception. Two larger rooms opening to the right and to the left off the hall were covered with mattresses and blankets, hot water was prepared, operation table opened out, and towels and instruments made ready. Just when we had about finished preparations our first arrivals, four men of the Dragoon Guards, turned up. They had been wounded slightly in the arms and face while advancing along the road towards Festubert. Twenty minutes later fifty-four wounded arrived, Bedfords and Cheshires, most of whom had slight wounds of the arms and hands and scalp, and were able to walk.

Urgent orders came in to send six ambulance waggons down the Festubert road. These were sent forward with stretcher parties and six medical officers. This was the beginning of a very "bloody" night. All that evening and all night wounded were continually coming in. I was on duty in the château as surgeon till 4 a.m., when another medical officer relieved me. Red Cross ambulances were driven up frequently and took away all our lightly wounded and those fit to travel. These were sent to Bethune, and thus the château was kept from becoming too congested. These Red Cross ambulances had been provided and equipped by British residents in Paris; they were splendidly handled, and proved a godsend to us. Many of them were converted "Ford cars," and could carry six lying-down patients and one sitting up beside the driver. The stretchers were swung on trestles and chains, and fitted easily. Our ambulance waggons and stretcher-bearers were out all night and had a very dangerous time at the front. At 10.30 next morning the heavy artillery firing eased off, and at eleven o'clock occurred one of those extraordinary lulls when all the big guns and little guns cease firing and everything seems strangely silent.

A chaplain arrived at the château in the morning and read the service over one of our wounded who had died during the night from a broken spine. The grave was dug near the flower garden at the foot of the lawn, and many graves were dug there in the three succeeding terrible weeks of fierce, bitter fighting. On this day the Dorsets, who were in reserve and quartered near the gate of our château, went into action and were badly handled by the Germans, suffering severe losses, chiefly from a concealed German machine-gun opening on to them from near the canal. The Devons had to move up later to support the Dorsets, and did it in a most gallant style. About two o'clock in the afternoon we had a great number of casualties; our waggons were constantly arriving, unloading their wounded, and setting off again for the front.

The Red Cross ambulances were evacuating the light cases as speedily as possible to Bethune, but we very soon had all our rooms full of wounded men and were working at high pressure at the operation table. At three o'clock the artillery firing was tremendously heavy, and every gun was in action. The château shook with the explosions; every window rattled and some were broken. The concussion of the air outside and the terrible din were distinctly unpleasant. Then the cracking of the rifle-firing became audible, and reports came in that our men were retiring. Shortly after an imperative order was sent to our O.C. telling him to evacuate the château at once with his wounded and move off the Field Ambulance to the other side of the canal. The horses were at once put in the various supply waggons. We had only two ambulance waggons at the time, as the rest were at the front collecting wounded. Some Red Cross ambulances, however, turned up and took away twelve of our most serious cases. All the lightly wounded were sent under charge of R.A.M.C. orderlies to walk back across the canal to Bethune.

Some men with shrapnel wounds of thigh and leg also had to walk and get along somehow, and miserable and pitiable these poor fellows looked, limping and struggling along the muddy road in their bloody bandages. Things looked pretty serious at this moment, and I was ordered to mount and gallop ahead to direct the waggons on to the right road and to "round up" our poor wounded fellows who were trudging along the roads. To make matters worse, heavy rain came on. Big artillery practice always brought down the rain. I soon reached the head of our column and gave the sergeant the necessary instructions.

On the side of the road there was an old inn or *estaminet.* I pulled my horse up here and put two men on duty to stop all our walking wounded and collect them into the front room of the inn. I went inside and arranged with the woman in charge to light a big fire, make some tea, and have bread and butter and anything else she could get ready for our men, and to do it quickly. She set to work at once. I had then to gallop back to the Château Gorre to help get away the serious cases and to collect any empty lorry or waggon I could get. When I reached the château the O.C. told me that we had moved up some reserves, and the Germans in their turn were now retiring. He said that he would now keep his serious cases at the château till motor ambulances arrived. I was ordered to gallop again to the head of our column and turn back all the supply waggons, equipment carts, and water carts, but to send the ambulance waggons with their wounded on to Bethune. It was now dark, and after incredible trouble my mission was accomplished and our drivers were already driving the carts back. I now looked in at "mine inn." All our wounded fellows were sitting round the fire having tea, bread and butter, and slices of cold boiled ham, and looked very happy. I asked thc woman of the inn what the cost was, and she only charged me ten francs. I never parted with money so willingly. The privilege of being able to do something for these good lads, and their appreciation of the hot fire and the hot tea, was something I would not willingly forget.

The Château Gorre was once more re-established as an advanced ambulance dressing station, and continued so for over three weeks. It was situated right inside the shell zone, and had many "alarms and excursions" during this period, but none quite so dramatic and sensational as that recorded above. The work done by this ambulance at the château was extraordinarily good and useful, and owing to its very advanced position so close to the fighting line it was able to receive and treat the wounded very soon after they had been hit.

When the order came to evacuate at the time of the incident related above, the instructions given to our Commanding Officer were to get out all the lightly wounded cases and to leave the serious cases in the château. Our O.C. was a soldier, and he said that if he had to go he would get all the wounded out, and that he would be "damned if he would leave any seriously wounded man in the hands of the b—— Germans." Strong language at times is sweet music, and our O.C. was a man of his word. The wounded men heard this story, and I heard some of them talking about it later to each other. The O.C. took a high place in their estimation.

At the château I was talking to a young lieutenant who had just received a commission in the D—— Regiment. He had served as a private at the beginning of the war and won his sergeant's stripes for general good conduct and gallantry under fire, and was then given a commission in another regiment. He was hard put for a smoke, and could not get any cigarettes, but fortunately I was able to give him some.

Ten days later, at Bethune, he was brought in to me with a crushed arm, hanging by only a thread of muscle to the shoulder, and I had to amputate it under chloroform. He recognised me as the man who had given him the cigarettes, and said, "Hullo, doctor, you're always doing me kind things, so now take my arm off." I was very sorry that I had to do it, but such is war and the aftermath of victory.

Next day after our big alarm I was sent back by the Assistant Director of the Medical Service of this Division to take up duty at Bethune, four miles back from where we were, at the Château Gorre, and to help in the organisation for handling and treating our many wounded there. Bethune was on the other side of the canal to the château, and during the succeeding three or four weeks became a very big hospital centre for the British engaged in the direction of La Bassée.

The Field Ambulance headquarters, with the waggons, still remained at the château closer to the firing line, and evacuated their many wounded as speedily as possible in to us at Bethune. These were strenuous days of hard and obstinate fighting, and the casualties were heavy. The life of the medical officer was at this place arduous and sleepless, but the motto of the Royal Army Medical Corps is " In arduis fidelis," which may be freely rendered " Always do your job."

CHAPTER XV.

BETHUNE.

Bethune held a position of great importance behind our lines, for our wounded were evacuated thither from the front, and those fit to take the journey were then sent on by hospital trains to Boulogne and Rouen and then to England. This old city will be visited by many English after the war, for many English officers and men are sleeping their long sleep in the old cemetery and in various parts of the surrounding country. One day, I am sure, a monument to the memory of the brave dead will be raised in Bethune, and the mural inscription will commemorate the names of the fallen, and place on record for all time the kindness, the sympathy, and the generous hearts of the people of Bethune who helped us all so much during the hard days of the war.

Owing to its many recent bombardments from guns and aeroplanes, and its proximity to the famous canal and La Bassée, Bethune has become a city of world-wide interest. Its population was at this time a cosmopolitan one. The warriors of the East were in friendly touch with the warriors of the West. The slanting, almond-eye Gurkha, the stately bearded Sikh, the swarthy fighting men from the frontiers and central plains of India, the Turcos with their flowing robes, the dapper Spahi, the black-eyed Senegalese, the French Alpine Chasseur, and the splendid Cuirassier, were all to be seen in its streets; and there also was Mr. Thomas Atkins, making himself, as usual, quite at home with them all, and also with the pleasant-faced smiling young women in the tobacconists and fruit shops.

Bethune, with its 14,000 inhabitants, is said to be the home of many millionaires—those manufacturing and industrial magnates who control the big industries of this thriving and populous part of France. The situation of the city is not very attractive. It is surrounded by muddy, swampy country, in some places nothing better than marshes or bogs in winter, but it is supposed to be attractive in spring and summer, when it is "a green prairie land."

The old square in the centre of the city has a very Flemish complexion, but is undoubtedly, owing to the irregularities in design and architecture of the surrounding houses and shops, a very attractive and fascinating spot. On one side are two fine old fourteenth-century Spanish houses built for some Spanish grandees in the days when Spain was supreme in the Netherlands. In the centre of the square is an old church and a mass of hoary buildings forming an island, and out of this island group of buildings the wonderful old Belfry of Bethune erects itself proudly skyward. The belfry was built in 1346, and behind it is the venerable church of St. Vaast, a product of the sixteenth century, with a very ornate Gothic tower.

Naturally the belfry and the tower of St. Vaast proved to be irresistibly attractive to the German gunners, and the batteries beyond La Bassée were constantly having long bowls practice at them. From the top of the belfry one could obtain a splendid view of the surrounding countryside and see the shrapnel and big shells burst miles away. Taubes were constantly flying over Bethune at this time, but later on they became very chary about visiting it.

The life of the old city during the past eight months has been rather unhappy, and it has gone through some stormy periods in the past. In 1188 a devastating plague swept the countryside, causing thousands of deaths and plunging the population into an abyss of fear and misery.

When the plague was at its height Saint Eloi appeared to two blacksmiths and recommended them to form an association of "charitables," charged to perform the last offices for the dead gratuitously and to help those in distress. This curious association exists to-day in Bethune under the name of Confrères des Charitables. During our stay in Bethune the charitables lived up to their old tradition and took the deepest interest in the welfare of our soldiers, made coffins for a very large number of our dead, and in their curious three-cornered "Napoleonic" hats and quaint badge and bands, solemnly followed the many dead to their last resting-place.

Bethune has passed through many sieges in its day. In 1487 it was in possession of the Germans under

Philippe of Cleves, and was captured by the French under Marshal d'Erquerdes at the victory called "Journée des Fromages," and at a later period of its history it was fortified by the great French engineer, Vauban.

The people of Bethune opened wide their arms and welcomed our wounded. From the Mayor of the city to the humblest little shop girl these good people did all they could for our men, dead, wounded, or active. The women of the town made delicacies, soups, and special dishes, provided wines and more solid comforts, such as beds, mattresses, blankets, and sheets. Had I but lifted my little finger and asked for volunteer nurses, I could, I am sure, have obtained them in hundreds. Every day while I was there I received letters from all sorts of people offering me help and all manner of things for our men. On an afternoon at Bethune at this time it was "the thing" for ladies to visit L'Hôpital Civil et Militaire and see the British soldiers. Our lightly wounded men would generally be sitting about on seats outside in the courtyard of the hospital surrounded by convalescent Frenchmen and crowds of admiring ladies, who had brought cigarettes, chocolate, and cakes for the soldiers of both nations.

Although Tommy did not know a word of French and they knew no English, they seemed to thoroughly understand each other, judging by the amused faces of the elder French ladies and the screams of laughter of the younger ones. We could never quite understand how Tommy has won such an enduring place in French hearts. The French people certainly like Tommy. I was glad to see this everywhere in France, for I, too, like Tommy, although he is full of tricks.

A section of the Field Ambulance consisting of two medical officers, Royal Army Medical Corps orderlies, waggons, cooks, and equipment had already taken possession of the school called L'École Jules Ferry, and was getting it into some order so as to act as a Clearing Hospital, or temporary Dressing Station or temporary Clearing Hospital.

We were to hold the fort till a properly equipped Clearing Hospital with its increased *personnel* and supplies should arrive. This did not appear for some days, and our Field Ambulance section had the herculean task of handling all the wounded from the fighting front, where a bloody struggle was in progress round the swamps and marshy country towards La Bassée. L'École Jules Ferry was situated down a side street of the old city, and near the railway station. It was a very large school, with several big lofty rooms, many small side-rooms, porches and alcoves of many sorts. There was a large courtyard with latrines, and the buildings formed a hollow square with part of the courtyard in the centre. The face of the buildings looking on to the courtyard had a long sweep of verandahs. The orderlies soon got to work, cleaned and swept the rooms, and covered the floor thickly with clean straw. No beds were then available. In a small side-room off a passage-way an operating table was fixed, and the surgical instruments and dressings were laid ready. Boiling water had to be carried to the operating room in buckets from the kitchen at the end of the building. The hospital was all very crude, but it was the best that could be done under the circumstances.

We did not have to await events; the events were there at once in the guise of crowds of recently wounded men. Motor ambulance after motor ambulance dashed up with its load of wounded. These were rapidly lifted out and carried into the building; then away went the ambulance to bring in more wounded. Many and large as were the schoolrooms they were quickly filled to overflowing. The corridors and porches were then covered with straw, and this straw was soon covered with rows of wounded men. The paved courtyard under the verandahs was covered with thick straw, and again covered with wounded. Every foot, every inch of floor space in the buildings and under the verandahs was utilised. In one room we had closely packed rows four deep, with a narrow footway of straw down the centre of the room for the doctors and orderlies to pass along. So narrow was this track, that it required the agility of a mountain goat to negotiate it without bumping some poor devil's feet, and we walked along it just as a man walks across a ploughed field, stepping high and watching each step. Those densely packed rooms during that long night were a lurid and impressive picture of the devastation of war. As more and more wounded continued to arrive we had to pack our men closer and closer together—gently push one this way, lift another one there, edge a third one closer still. So it went on. We had in our rooms a number of French wounded picked up and brought in by our ambulances, and also a fair number of German wounded. There is no nationality amongst the men in a hospital, and English, French, and German all had a little bit of floor space and a bit of straw in our schoolhouse that night. All were glad to get in out of the pouring rain, and be placed on the warm dry straw, and covered with a blanket.

All these men arrived with the first field-dressings on. Some had been put on by the surgeon with the regiment, some by bearers and orderlies, some by Field Ambulance officers, and some by the man's comrades on the field.

At first we were so busy "packing" our wounded that we could not investigate the nature of the wounds, but we were very soon under way with the professional side of our work. Every wound was examined; the slight ones were left alone, but the serious ones were re-dressed and a rough differentiation of serious and slight cases was made. Those requiring immediate surgery were brought into our operation room and anæsthetics were administered. All men in pain were given hypodermics of morphia, and our orderlies made hot drinks and soups for all those able to take nourishment. There were, of course, many men lying unconscious with severe brain wounds, and most of these men died next day. The brain injuries were amongst our most hopeless cases, but fortunately these poor fellows suffered no pain whatever, and slept stertorously till death. There was one particularly fine, strapping, young giant lieutenant of a Scotch regiment who was comfortably placed on straw and covered with a blanket, and who lay quietly sleeping, with gentle and easy respirations, all the night till the next forenoon, when he suddenly became quite still. The top of his head had been blown completely away.

The crowds of wounded behaved like brave men and took their gruelling like good sportsmen. Next day the pressure was relieved by the opportune arrival of a hospital train, and we were enabled to evacuate 250 of the cases fit for transport. More doctors and Red Cross dressers were sent to help, and the vacant places of the 250 sent away were occupied by the arrival of another 300.

As the pressure for beds showed no signs of easing off, and as the reports from the front were that the fighting was still violent and obstinate, a search was made for another building to hold more wounded. This was found at L'Hôpital Civil et Militaire, a permanent hospital of the city of Bethune. It was a hospital of three stories, built of brick round three sides of a big hollow square. The fourth side was occupied by the porter's lodge, the two gateways, and the residential quarters of the Reverend Mother and Sisters of the Order of St. Francis, who formed the nursing staff. The basement wards of one wing were for French military patients, and the other wings were for civilian patients; but as a matter of fact military wounded were put in all the wards except the midwifery ward, which was full of young babies and mothers. One of these young mothers, by the way, had just become the proud possessor of triplets. I had a look at them, and they seemed very fit. Their father had been away for the past three months in the trenches of the Argonne, but permission had been asked to enable him to come down and see how well his wife had done.

The top story of the hospital had two large empty wards, each capable of holding seventy patients placed fairly closely together. I asked permission of the Reverend Mother and the hospital secretary to use these wards for the reception of our wounded.

"But yes," I was eagerly told; "you are welcome, and we shall do all we can for your English wounded." I was also offered the use of three side-rooms and part of another small ward for any wounded officers, and—greatest boon of all—the use of the two operating theatres of the hospital. These operating theatres were modern and splendidly equipped with good surgical iron operating tables, suitable for adjusting in any position, sterilisers for instruments, dressings, aprons, and operating towels, glass cases full of the latest type of instruments, and hot and cold water taps controlled by foot-pedals on the floor.

The lighting was all that one could desire. My joy knew no bounds now, for I felt that at last I would be able to do good surgery and clean surgery. Up till now the surgery I had done on the field was crude and not very clean. It was absolutely impossible to be otherwise, for we were the victims of stern military circumstances. But now things would be different, and our wounded men and officers would get the benefit of surgical cleanliness.

I asked the Reverend Mother if she would prepare one hundred straw mattresses for me, and get in some blankets. "But yes" I would get them; and also Monsieur le Docteur would have tables put in the centre of the wards for the dressings, and would have basins and towels. An electrician would fix up electric lights, and a kitchen stove would be put in a side-room for cooking soup, boiling water, etc. I reported all this to Surgeon-General P——, and that able officer quickly grasped the possibilities of this hospital, installed me there as operating surgeon, and directed that all serious cases requiring surgical operation should be sent to me. A real Clearing Hospital arrived in the town next morning, and next day took in patients. It established itself in the "College for Young Ladies," and very soon the spacious quarters of this big building were filled with wounded and sick men. For besides our wounded at this time we had also a large number of sick. This hospital also sent me any case requiring surgical operation.

Work at my wards proceeded apace. The women of the city rushed eagerly to assist, and in a *clin d'œil* had made 180 straw mattresses, provided blankets, hot-water bottles, and other sick-room adjuncts. The position in Bethune was now as follows. One Clearing Hospital at the College for Young Ladies, one at the school "Jules Ferry," and my surgical wards, only for serious cases, at L'Hôpital Civil et Militaire. All three buildings were soon full, and over seven thousand wounded men passed through these buildings in less than three weeks.

Sir Anthony Bowlby, consulting surgeon to the Army, constantly visited this hospital, and was always a welcome visitor; and his surgical opinion was as welcome as his encouragement and cheeriness of manner.

The operating theatre was presided over by Sister Ferdinande, a trained and capable nurse, with rigid antiseptic and aseptic principles. All I had to do was to tell her that I was going to amputate a limb or do a trephining operation, and ask her when she would be ready. At the agreed time everything was certain to be prepared, and I just had to scrub up, put on my sterilised apron, cap, and rubber gloves, and be ready for my part of the *séance*. The Reverend Mother Superior was a trained anæsthetist and administered chloroform to many of my cases during the three weeks I was there. Some days I have had her administering anæsthetics for seven hours. Seven hours' continuous administration, broken only by the taking out of one patient and the bringing in of another, is a big test of endurance for a young man; yet this old lady did it smilingly and well, and said it was "indeed nothing."

There were two Irish nuns at this hospital; one spoke French well, one was just learning, but both spoke "Irish," which is good English. These two nuns were put on nursing duty in my wards, and they were hugely delighted to get amongst the British wounded and to hear their countrymen talk. Tommy Atkins was delighted with the two Irish nuns, and told them some wonderful stories about the fighting and about the Germans. One of them asked me if I really thought that Private S—— of the Warwicks had shot two hundred Germans one afternoon. I told the sister that I did not know, but hoped he had. These two sisters were at work in the wards night and day. They told me one day that they had never heard a soldier swear. I was very glad to hear this, for it showed that Tommy was behaving himself, and I did not tell the sister that Tommy on occasion was a very past master in strange oaths. The sisters were very concerned about the lice on our soldiers' shirts and flannels; and really this was a terrible source of anxiety to all medical officers at this time, for these cursed parasites would make the lot of our wounded men unbearable at times. One man with a fractured leg put up firmly in splints begged me to take the splints off so that he could "scratch the leg." I had really in the end to take off the splint, bathe the skin in petrol, and dust sulphur on the cotton wool, for lice had worked their way down into the warm wool next the skin, and by their "promenading" about had set up the irritation which the soldier begged to scratch. The sister once said to me that she used to think that the British soldiers were the most cleanly of men, but she found really that they were all covered with lice.

I told the wondering-eyed sister that it was a regrettable fact, but nevertheless true, that the whole British Army at the front was lousy.

When our wounded arrived at the hospital they were speedily placed on the straw mattresses, quickly undressed by the sisters and other helping nuns, and covered with warm sheets and blankets and surrounded with hot bottles. Basins of hot water and soap were brought round and then the men were washed and cleaned. Their lice-infected shirts and underclothing were sterilised by dry heat.

It was the finest example of *l'entente cordiale* to see the French nuns taking off the muddy boots and puttees, cutting off blood-stained clothing, washing and cleaning the wounded, slipping on warm dry shirts, and tucking the blankets and pillows comfortably. Others appeared with hot soup, hot coffee, red wine, and hot gruel. These nuns were magnificent.

I wrote to Lord Grey, late Governor-General of Canada, asking him to bring to the notice of Her Majesty Queen Alexandra the splendid work performed by these ladies. Lord Grey very kindly did so, and also sent a copy of my letter to His Majesty the King, who replied through Lord Stamfordham that he had read it with much interest. Queen Alexandra sent the following letter to the Reverend Mother Superior of the Franciscan Sisters at Bethune:

"I have learned from Dr. Martin of your noble and heroic devotion for our brave and unfortunate wounded soldiers, and it is with a heart full of gratitude that I ask you to accept my most ardent and warmest thanks.

"I pray God that He will reward you for the angelic care that you have bestowed on our unfortunate soldiers, and I will never forget that it is to you, madame, and your sisters, that they assuredly owe their life and their recovered health.

"ALEXANDRA."

This letter was published in all the leading French and British papers, including the *London Times*, *Tablet*, *Daily Mail*, *Figaro*, *Le Journal*, *Le Temps*, in February 1915, and excited very considerable interest and attention in France. The Abbé Bouchon d'Homme, the Aumonier to the hospital, wrote me later to say that the Reverend Mother and the Sisters were delighted beyond measure at Queen Alexandra's gracious message.

It may not be out of place now to describe briefly the nature of some of the wounds met with during the fighting at La Bassée. The non-medical mind is as interested in the wounds and sufferings of our men as are the doctors, and it is to the intelligent interest of the layman we owe so much of what has been done for our wounded and sick men. Compound fractures and splintered bone, septic wounds, tetanus, brain injuries, inoculations, etc., are words freely bandied about and understood by any group of ladies met together round an afternoon tea-table. Mrs. Smith-Jones will tell Mrs. Jones-Smith that her son is in hospital with a septic compound fracture and that the wound is being fully drained, and Mrs. J.-S. will reply that her sister's husband, Captain X—— of the R.F.A., is recovering from a penetrating wound of the lung, but has still some pleural effusion. So no apology is further necessary when referring to such a thing as gas gangrene.

Gas gangrene was one of the terrors of the doctors at this time. It was a new and totally unexpected complication of the wounds, and at first we did not know what to do in the face of this pressing danger. A man would get, say, a flesh wound of the arm or leg, or perhaps a fractured bone, and very soon the whole limb would become gangrenous and die. Gangrene means death of the part. It may be death of a small part or of a large part, and the worst feature of the form of gangrene met with at Bethune was its tendency to rapid spread, resulting in the speedy death of the limb and of the patient. We had many deaths from this terrible gas gangrene, and performed many amputations to save lives. A good surgeon hates to amputate a limb, and will gladly exert all his skill and knowledge to save even a toe. It was heartrending to have to perform so many amputations at Bethune, and yet these serious mutilating operations had to be performed in order to save lives.

The gangrene was caused by a group of bacilli called anærobes, amongst which may be many organisms. About ten different organisms have been obtained from cases of gas gangrene, and these all belong to the same family of anærobic bacilli. They are all spore-bearing, and grow in the absence of air. These bacilli are found in the soil in France and Belgium, and are always to be found in the soil of those countries which have been closely cultivated for centuries past.

If a guinea-pig is inoculated with a sample of this earth shaken up in a little water it will develop this gas gangrene and die. Imagine, then, this picture. The soil of the trenches is full of these organisms, which, if introduced into an open wound, grow and spread and cause the limb to become gangrenous. As the organism spreads up the limb it produces a gas of its own, and by pressing on the skin one can feel this gas cracking, like tissue paper, under the fingers. The treatment is to inject the parts with oxygen or peroxide of hydrogen, to make free incisions round the wound, thoroughly cleanse the wound and keep it clean. The general condition of the patients required great care, for they were all very, very ill. When a man got wounded in the trenches some dirt was bound to get into the wound, for the men's hands and clothes were usually caked with mud.

It is a natural movement to clap a hand on the wounded spot. If a man is struck on the face or limbs, he will lay down his rifle or perhaps drop it, and at once put his hand on the injured part to ascertain the extent. It is a movement which is almost involuntary. I have seen hit men do this often, and when they withdraw their hand they always look at it to see if there is any blood, and the bravest man does not like to see his own blood. The hands of the men in the trenches were infected with the bacilli of this gas gangrene and of tetanus, and when these infected fingers touched a recent wound, the wound itself became infected with these highly dangerous organisms.

Pieces of khaki cloth, caked in mud, were often driven into the wounds with the bullets and shrapnel, and on this cloth there were of course millions of the deadly little beasts.

If the case reached us soon after the onset of gangrene a cure could almost certainly be promised. If the case arrived late, when the limbs were dead, amputation was the only "conservative treatment" that one could adopt. Many of the cases sent to me were beyond any hope of recovery and soon died. On one day I saw in one Clearing Hospital in the town four cases dying from gas gangrene; in the other Clearing Hospital, two cases *in articulo mortis* from the same trouble; and in my own, one other case. Seven cases dying on one day from gas gangrene! None of these had been operated upon. This will give some idea of the formidable character of this complication.

None but the very serious cases were sent to me. Many cases of gas gangrene were evacuated early and sent to the Base Hospitals. Most of my cases came from one or other of the Clearing Hospitals in this town. Some arrived direct from the Field Ambulances. In every amputation for gas gangrene performed at this hospital the limb was absolutely dead and beyond the possibility of any treatment short of amputation. All the patients were in an extremely grave state, and their general condition was in every case very bad. I cannot picture any worse surgical subject than these men with gas gangrene. Numbers of them were in too low a state to admit of a general anæsthetic, and here the necessary operations were performed under conduction anæsthesia.

Dr. F——, an eminent French surgeon in charge of the French wounded in this town, saw many of my cases before, during, and after operation. I had the privilege also of seeing his gangrene cases at this time. He had amongst the French wounded the same experience as mine. Both of us had German wounded to treat, and here also we met dead limbs from gas gangrene. We were both of the opinion that the Germans at this place were also up against a very virulent "culture" here, that of the anærobe. Some wounded French refugees were brought into this hospital at this period, and some of these had gas gangrene. The serious character of gas gangrene at this time could only be recognised at the front. The serious cases were retained here for operation. I am of the opinion that all cases of gangrene should be treated at the front at the nearest Clearing Hospital, and that no case should be sent to the Base till the gangrene had disappeared, subject, of course, as always, to the military situation. All the wounded admitted to this town—French, British, and German—came from the same area of the battle front.

In many of the cases of gas gangrene bones were badly shattered and pulverised, splinters of bone were lying in surrounding muscles, or had been driven out through the skin. Important nerves were injured, torn, or compressed in many of them. Important blood-vessels were frequently, but not invariably, injured. In some, big vessels had been torn through; in others, arteries and nerves were compressed by displaced fragments of bone. The wounds were dirty in most cases. The skin was black and lacerated, and muscles were extruded and covered with coagulated blood clots.—Wound full of blood clots, and containing at times pieces of khaki cloth, shrapnel fragments, nickel casing of bullets, gravel, and, in two cases, bits of rock.—So runs the record in my notes. There were, however, cases in which the bullet had drilled an apparently clean hole through a joint, like the wrist or ankle, without much apparent destruction to bone. In such cases one would not expect gas gangrene; yet it sometimes occurred.

Gas gangrene is encouraged by tight bandaging, and many of the cases had a bandage applied all too firmly. When a man is wounded in a trench his mate frequently applies the first-aid dressing, and fixes it like a tourniquet. This could perhaps be obviated by making the bandage of the first field-dressing a little wider than at present. A narrow bandage tends to become cord-like.

All the cases of gas gangrene had a very penetrating putrefactive smell, which is quite characteristic. The area of advancing gangrene is preceded by an œdematous zone, which fades in one direction to the area of healthy skin and in the direction towards the wound to a dullish injected area which crackles on palpation. Nearer the wound the skin is purplish and dark. Around the edges of the usually jagged wound the tissues were black or greenish-black. Extravasated blood undermined the skin all round the wound. The wound itself was full of blood clots. The limb distal to the wound was swollen, greenish-black, covered with green blebs, cold, insensitive, and pulseless in the "dead" limbs. Frequently toes and fingers were quite black. In other serious cases there might be a little warmth or a slight pulse. If any case showed either of these two favourable signs, an attempt was made to save the limb, and was in many cases successful. The gangrene did not spread up a limb in an even circle. For example, it might reach anteriorly to the lower third of the thigh, and posteriorly be at or well above the fold of the buttock. This was due to the extravasated blood lying more towards the dependent parts and to gravity. In the upper arm the gangrene travelled rapidly up the inner side along the course of the big blood-vessels. The invasion spread upwards; very little crackling was felt below the site of the wound. The circulation below seemed to be rapidly cut off, and that portion of the limb underwent the changes associated with a complete circulatory block. Wounds of the thigh with shattering of the femur, wounds of the elbow-joint and of the metatarsus were very prone to develop this gangrene. Some of the cases were admitted within thirty-six hours after receipt of the wound, with well-marked gangrene.

In every case of amputation performed there was

nothing else to be done in order to save life. The limbs were dead. In many of these cases important blood-vessels were torn, crushed, or compressed, and when the vessels were injured the gangrene developed more quickly and spread more rapidly. It is regrettable that one had to perform so many amputations at this time, but it is a matter for congratulation that so many lives were saved. One of the cases died suddenly twelve hours after a disarticulation at the shoulder-joint. Another one died three days after amputation at the hip-joint, from gangrene which progressed steadily on to the lower abdomen. There were, in addition, five deaths from gangrene following wounds of the extremities. These five were admitted in a dying condition, and passed away two to four hours after admission. One could do nothing for them surgically. Other cases died at the other Clearing Hospitals in the town. It was a sad and mournful experience seeing these fine young men die.

These cases of gas gangrene were all bad surgical subjects, for in addition to the gangrene, loss of blood, privation, and exposure subsequent to being wounded, their wounds were dangerous and mutilating, and the transportation to the hospital was, sometimes, necessarily an agonising ordeal. This will show that our Clearing Hospitals at the front should be well and thoroughly equipped with all modern appliances for the treatment of shock, and a staff fully alive to this clamant necessity. A Clearing Hospital cannot to-day remain as an administrative unit only.

Another complication of our wounds at this time was tetanus (or the so-called lock-jaw). When it was recognised that the bacillus of tetanus was also found in the soil of France and Flanders, efficient measures were at once adopted to combat its terrible effects. Accordingly anti-tetanic serum was provided at all the Base Hospitals, Clearing Hospitals, and Ambulances, and every man wounded in France or Flanders to-day gets an injection of this serum within twenty-four hours of the receipt of the wound. No deaths from tetanus have occurred since these measures have been adopted.

Tetanus caused many deaths at the beginning of the war, not only amongst our own soldiers, but also amongst the Belgians, French, and Germans. When tetanus manifests itself, when the convulsions and muscular spasms come on, it is a terrible malady to treat, and most of the cases die. At this time the injection of anti-tetanic serum does not ensure a recovery, but if this serum is given to every wounded man, then none will develop tetanus, and that is why none of the wounded men are asked if they will have the "lock-jaw injection." At the front there is no time for conscientious objectors.

Shrapnel wounds were always bad; the round bullets of lead always ripped and tore the tissues about so terribly. The Mauser bullet did not cause nearly so much damage, but it sometimes produced very lacerating wounds. The Mauser bullet "turns over" when travelling through a limb, and this turning means tearing of tissues on the path of the bullet, and often a huge jagged wound like that produced by an explosive bullet.

It has been said that we are treating wounds of an eighteenth-century character with twentieth-century technique. The eighteenth-century battle wounds were inflicted at close range, and so are many of the wounds inflicted to-day.

At Crecy and Agincourt both sides used arrows. The aviators of the Allies and the enemy carry steel darts which they spin down on the foe below. Bows have been used in the trenches to send inflammable arrows into the opposing lines. The Roman soldier advanced to close combat behind a shield held on his left arm, and shields have been used at certain observation spots by the Germans and in the Russian trenches; our Allies have at times used spades for a similar purpose.

Bombards were employed at Crecy, and bombards have come to their own again in the trenches from Switzerland to the sea. Hand grenades were employed in the Peninsular War, and are employed to-day in this War of the Nations. Our men attack the enemy and the enemy attack us with bayonets as in the days of the Crimea and the Peninsula, and our riflemen pick off the enemy by long-distance fire, and also fire at close range into solid masses of them. Even the armour of old days is represented on modern fields of battle, for the French Cuirassier goes into action with a brass cuirass and helmet; and a French infantry officer of my acquaintance has worn a light shirt of chain-mail extending from his neck to beyond his hips, all through

13

this campaign, and he said that it had saved his life on more than one occasion. In one *magasin* in Rouen shirts of beautifully made chain-mail can be purchased, and the shopkeeper told me that he had sold hundreds to French soldiers.

The hardships of the Crimean trenches—cold, rheumatism, and frostbite—have been repeated on the Yser. Gangrene was rampant amongst the wounded of Wagram, Austerlitz, and Borodino, and amongst the French and British wounded at Vittoria, Salamanca, Badajos, and other great battles of the Peninsula, and it has startlingly reappeared on the Aisne and in Flanders.

Historians of that day refer to it as hospital gangrene, or the gangrene so common after any surgical operation or wound of that time. It may, on the other hand, have been the same gas gangrene that has ominously complicated so many of our wounds in France and Flanders. The bacillus which produces this gangrene may belong, for all we know to the contrary, to a very old family of bacilli, who would look upon pedigrees dating to William the Conqueror with an aristocratic contempt when his own stretched back to the beginning of time.

There is one feature of war as carried on to-day which is quite new, and that is by poison gases and by poisoning wells and water supplies. In West Africa the Germans have been proved indisputably and by their own admissions to have poisoned wells and water supplies, and the whole world stands amazed and aghast at the devilish and inhuman Germans who set free poison gases to overwhelm and suffocate British, French, and Belgian soldiers in the trenches. This diabolical and ghastly method of murder is without parallel in history, and the bloodily-minded men who conceived and carried out this sinister, ferocious thing will live accursed all their days and be a name of scorn and loathing for ever.

Although the civil hospital at Bethune was such a grim place of crowded wounded, it was yet the scene of much humour. We had wounded men belonging to many different countries, and the nuns were very interested in all the odd types. Off one of the large French wards there was a small room holding eight beds, and a nun brought me in one day to see the curious occupants ranged in beds alongside each other. There were a Senegalese, an Algerian, a Zouave, an Alpine Chasseur, a Turco, a native of Madagascar, a man of the Foreign legion, and a Frenchman. I think that the nuns always kept this ward " International." It was their little joke, and visitors were always shown this ward. The patients themselves enjoyed the *mélange.* The courtyard of the hospital was a great meeting-place for our convalescent soldiers with the French convalescents, and they used to sit about on benches surrounded by an admiring lot of French women from the town. We also had a fair number of German wounded on our hands, and one of them at this time was terribly ill, suffering from the after-effects of gas gangrene of the foot following on a bullet wound of the ankle joint. His foot was amputated, and he had a struggle for some days to keep going, but eventually pulled through. The wounded German soldiers were very tractable and easy to manage. They were obedient, gave no trouble, and seemed grateful. I cannot say the same of the two wounded German officers I had. Both were slight wounds, and ought not really to have been sent to this hospital at all. They were truculent and overbearing to the nuns and orderlies, and behaved like cads. The German has no sense of humour. He takes himself very seriously, and that amuses us. He thinks and says that we are fools, and that also amuses us. A German once said that the English would always be fools, and that the Germans would never be gentlemen. This is most obviously correct. We asked a German sergeant-major who had been captured if the Hymn of Hate was really popular in Germany. The sergeant-major in civil life was a school teacher. He wore big spectacles and had a rough beard, and was altogether a very serious-minded man. He assured us that the German hate was a very real one, and he took the hymn very seriously. Lissauer, its author, is said to be a serious man also, and has he not been awarded the Cross of the Red Eagle by the All Highest himself? We laugh at the hymn, and this makes the German mad. Certainly we must be fools to laugh at the Hymn of Hate. The words inspire and enthral the Teuton, and the music uplifts his sentimental soul to the Empyrean.

> "We love as one, we hate as one.
> We have one foe, and one alone—England."

The German considers this to be a purely German hymn, breathing the spirit of the Fatherland—unending hate. It is his song, and to sing it does him good. You can then understand the expression of blank amazement on the face of our captured schoolmaster—the sergeant-major with the spectacles and beard—when he was told that the Hymn of Hate was sung with gusto in the music halls of London and Paris, and was received by the audience with shrieking sounds of applause.

The Hymn of Hate sung by an Englishman in an English music hall! Donnerwetter! He could not understand. He had no sense of humour.

A Prussian officer was captured in November with about fifteen men, and I saw him marched in shortly after the capture. He looked arrogant, and one instinctively took a dislike to him, he was so obviously stamped "bounder."

His revolver was in its pouch on his belt. We had forgotten to take it, and he had forgotten that it was there. Our prisoner spoke English very well, and said that "he wished he had been shot. He was for ever and ever disgraced at being made a prisoner. His regiment would not have him again as an officer." The impression we formed, who were standing round listening, was that this whining bounder seemed to feel it a particular disgrace to be a prisoner of the hated English. An English officer in charge at this particular place here went up to our snarling Prussian who wished "that he had been killed" and said: "I see we have omitted to take over your revolver. It is still in your pouch and probably loaded—sure to be. You say you are sorry you were not killed. Well, go off five paces over there and blow your damned head off with your own gun. I won't interfere with you, and none of us will mourn for you." The Prussian shut up like an oyster. We all laughed, and the soldiers round enjoyed it hugely. The eyes of the man blazed with fury, but he made no movement towards that five paces off, and handed over his revolver to our English officer, who refused to touch it, and called on a soldier to take it.

The Prussian did not see the humour of the situation, and "there's the humour on't" old Falstaff would have said.

A few days after the sinking of the *Emden* the news reached the British and French in the trenches. The French were as delighted as we were. In the Argonne an advanced French trench was separated by only the width of a road from an advanced German trench. The officer in command of the French trench wrote out the news of the *Emden* fight on a piece of paper and tied this paper round a stone, which he flung into the German trench. It was received with guttural cries of annoyance. Shortly after this time from the German trench came another stone with a piece of paper inscribed, "Monsieur, go to Hell." The French officer, ever polite and determined to have the last word, sent back this note :

"DEAR BOSCHES,—I have been to many places. I

have been invited to visit many places in my time, but this is the first time that I have been invited to visit the German headquarters."

There is a society in London called the "Society for Lonely Soldiers." Its object is to be of some assistance to soldiers who have no relations or friends and are quite alone in the world. A young lady of this society sent a parcel of comforts to the British prison camp in Germany, and addressed the parcel to "The loneliest British soldier in Germany."

Some weeks afterwards a reply was received from the German officer in command of the camp. "Madam, your gifts have been impartially distributed amongst all the prisoners. We were unable to decide which was the *loveliest* British soldier in camp." Imagine a spectacled old German officer methodically scrutinising all the British prisoners to ascertain which was the "loveliest" one!

Apropos of humour, read this incident reported by "Eye-witness" from the front. "One wounded Prussian officer of a particularly offensive and truculent type, which is not uncommon, expressed the greatest contempt for our methods: 'You do not fight. You murder!' he said. 'If it had been straightforward, honest fighting we should have beaten you, but my regiment never had a chance from the first. There was a shell every ten yards. Nothing could live in such a fire.'"

This from one of the apostles of frightfulness!

Now read this concluding sentence in a letter from a German lady of high social position to a Russian lady:

"We wish to carry in our hearts an undying hatred, and we utterly reject all useless verbiage on 'humanity.'

"To mothers and to German women this hate gives a sort of satisfaction without which our hearts would not be able to support," etc. etc.

Read this order of the day, dated 26th August 1914, from General Stenger, Brigadier of the 88th Brigade, 14th Baden Army Corps. (This document is quite authentic, and is at present in the hands of the French War Office.) This is the translation: "The Brigade on setting out to-day will make no prisoners; all prisoners will be killed. The wounded, with or without arms, will be put to death. Prisoners, even in large organised units, will be put to death. No living man must remain in our rear."

More will be heard of this document at the end of the war. It is a prized possession of the French just now.

Yet our wounded Prussian officer, as related above, objected to our murderous artillery fire, and said that "we do not fight, we murder." In spite of the tragic side the incident has some humour.

Dr. Ludwig Ganghofer, a Bavarian Court journalist, recently described a visit which he had paid to a German hospital in Lille. He there saw some wounded British prisoners. Two caught his eye, and thus he writes:

"As I regarded these two sulky pups of the British lion, I had a feeling as if every hair on my head stood on end. This unpleasant irritation only ceased when I had turned my German back on the sons of civilised Albion, and looked again at suffering human beings."

"Suffering human beings" is good; our two unfortunate countrymen were not human beings. They were pups of the British lion—young lions, in fact. The German appellation for us is improving. Some weeks ago we were "Swine dogs," now we are "Young lions." Ganghofer is the Bavarian Court journalist. One wonders if that feudal power keeps a court jester.

CHAPTER XVI.

SOME MEDICAL ODDS AND ENDS.

FUNCTIONAL BLINDNESS.

AT Bethune some of us met for the first time in this war cases of functional temporary blindness, and many other cases were met with at various points of the front.

The following example will give an idea of the condition. A young officer, nineteen years of age, was standing by a haystack in the north of France when a large Black Maria burst near him, rolled him over, and plastered him with clay, but did not kill him. The *concussion* had thrown him down. He remained unconscious for half an hour, and when he woke to consciousness he discovered he was " blind." His mental state then was terrible. He cried out, " Oh, why wasn't I killed ? " " Won't some one carry me out and put me on the parapet of a trench so that I may be killed ? " His grief was pathetic, and one can easily understand it. A careful examination was made of the interior of the eyes with the ophthalmoscope and nothing was found wrong. He was assured by the medical officers that he would certainly recover after perhaps a week or two of blindness. He was quiet and composed after this, but was a little bit suspicious that we were only trying to cheer him up. One medical officer then explained to him what sort of blindness it was: that it was due to concussion of the nerve of sight, and the delicate structures at the ball of the eye; that nothing was destroyed, and that a complete rest would bring back his vision. Next day he was transferred by hospital train to the Base *en route* for England. This note, unknown to him, was pinned on his coat: "Functional blindness. Any medical officer handling this officer on Hospital Train, Base Hospital, or Hospital Ship, please tell him that he will fully recover his sight." Knowing the kind-hearted nature of the medical profession, one can be sure that he was cheered up all the way to England. I received a letter from this officer's mother some weeks after, saying that her son had completely recovered his vision, and was as well as ever.

NERVE CONCUSSION

Nerve concussion is a pathological condition that has received more attention in this war than at any previous time. A young Fusilier at La Bassée was hit by a bullet through the fleshy part of the forearm. The wound was a purely flesh one and no important nerve could have been struck. He had paralysis of the wrist and hand, due to concussion of the important nerves of the forearm. The bullet in its course did not strike these nerves. He got completely better in eight weeks.

A Gordon Highlander was struck by a bullet in the

right buttock. No important nerve was struck, yet he had paralysis of the limb owing to concussion of the sciatic nerve. He got better by rest in bed and massage of the muscles. A soldier of the Wiltshire Regiment was rolled over by the concussion of a bursting shell. He retained consciousness, but could not get up or move his right arm. The right side of his body was paralysed. He got better by rest. A Bedfordshire sergeant got a bullet wound through the upper arm, and paralysis of certain muscles supplied by nerves in the vicinity of the track of the bullet. It was thought that the nerves were divided, and after the wound had healed the nerves were exposed at an operation intending to join the severed ends. The nerves were found to be uninjured, and the incision in the skin was closed up. He made a complete recovery.

There is also the story of the soldier who suddenly recovered his voice in the presence of King George. The story is going the rounds of the hospitals, and it is said that His Majesty was extraordinarily interested in the phenomenon. This soldier was taken prisoner by the Germans during our retreat from Belgium. He was picked off the field in a dazed condition and unable to speak. He was interned later in a prison camp in Germany and was all this time quite unable to speak. When the exchange of permanently disabled prisoners of war was recently made between England and Germany, this man was sent back as permanently incapacitated on account of being dumb. He was admitted to a hospital near London. One day the

King visited the hospital, and this man on getting up from his chair as the King entered the ward, inadvertently touched a heating pipe which was then very hot. He at once exclaimed " Damn," and was able to speak perfectly afterwards. The King was very much interested. Was this an hysterical loss of voice or a concussion? It was a mental shock of some kind, and the recovery was due to the other shock of touching a hot pipe.

I attended one young officer and three men who had been buried in the earth when their trench was blown up. The officer and one man were unconscious, and when the man recovered consciousness he was nervy and excitable. He had a startled, terrified expression, and when in bed he would peer round in a wild, anxious way, and then suddenly pull the blankets well over his head and curl up underneath as if anxious to shut out his surroundings, or what he thought were his surroundings. He seemed really to be living through some terrifying experiences of the past few days antecedent and up to the time when his trench was blown up and he was engulfed in the mud and *débris*.

The officer recovered consciousness more slowly, and spoke in a curious staccato speech; his nerves were completely gone, and he had fine tremors of the lips aud tongue and fingers. He told me that his memory had gone, that he had only a hazy recollection of recent things, which seemed far away and dim.

DEAF MUTISM.

Several cases of deaf mutism have occurred during the hard fighting near Ypres and La Bassée, and these are certainly very curious. The men so afflicted have written down that shells burst near them, that they were thrown down, and remembered nothing more for a time. On coming to again, they were deaf and dumb. These men also show other signs of nerve shock; they are restless, troubled with sleeplessness, and have anxious expressions. Generally all get completely well in a few weeks, but some of the cases remain mute for a much longer time.

LICE.

The medical officer at the front to-day has other duties besides those of attending to the sick and wounded. He is concerned with the prevention of disease, with water supplies, sanitation of billeting areas and camps, means to prevent frostbite, and so on. He has also to advise on methods of treating and avoiding vermin. Lice are, without a doubt, one of the terrors of war. These little beasts are not harmless. They take a high place in the sphere of destructive agents. I would group them in the class with shrapnel bombs and high explosives. Wherever many men are gathered closely together, and hygienic laws, owing to military needs, are in temporary abeyance, there will lice be found, constituting themselves one of the terrors of war. Officers and men get them, and once these pests gain entry to one's wardrobe they entrench themselves in their battalions and divisions, and require very drastic efforts to dislodge. In the early fighting in Flanders and in Northern France, on the Marne and Aisne, these beasts gave us great trouble. They are most active at night when one gets warm in bed. It is not the bite that counts, but, as the old French Countess once expressed it to a Minister of State, it is "toujours le promenade." The promenading causes irritation and insomnia. Scratching produces excoriations of the skin, and then a whole lot of sequent complications. Lice are factors in the spread of typhus fever, and when typhus visits an army in the field it carries death and desolation to thousands. To illustrate the point read this extract from a letter written from an English hospital in Serbia: "The great scourge of this country is typhus fever. It was introduced by the Austrian prisoners at Christmas. Out of 2500 Austrian prisoners at Uskub, 1000 had died of fever and 1200 were down with it. It is a terrible disease, and is carried not by infection but by lice. One has to take tremendous precautions to avoid these creatures."

The majority of our wounded taken from the fighting line at La Bassée to the hospital at Bethune were infested with lice. Lice invaded the clothing of all who handled these poor fellows, and very drastic measures had to be taken to combat the scourge.

The following story will illustrate the vitality of these nasty little beasts. Our Field Ambulance once stopped at a small town in Northern France and was billeted in a French convent. The good sisters allowed us the use of the schoolrooms, the kitchen, and some of the bedrooms. All the officers were anxious to get their shirts and linen washed. The laundrywoman duly appeared and boiled all these articles, and the sisters ironed them for us. On the afternoon of the ironing the Mother Superior and two sisters came to us in a state of excitement, talking rapidly, and evidently overcome with amazement. They explained that our shirts had been boiled and then dried in the open air. When they began to iron the necks of our shirts the lice sprang to life and were exceedingly active. They assured us solemnly that scores sprang to active life under the comfortable warmth of the hot iron. I do not doubt the story. The heat had matured the chitinous envelope in which the young lice lay, and out they came, joyous, active, and sportive on the nice warm surface. Hence the amazement, the uplifted hands, and the consternation of the good sisters. The riddle of their extermination has not yet been completely solved, but measures are in active progress. It is an unsavoury subject, but it is a very important one for troops in camp and in the field.

SHELL FUMES.

"Thou shalt not kill,
But do not strive
Officiously to keep alive."

A great deal has been written on the effect of shell fumes in this war. So much is hearsay and so little really authentic, that one cannot dogmatise.

One naval surgeon said that men exposed to fumes of bursting shells develop acute pneumonia, which proves fatal as a rule. This is supposed to be due to the nitric peroxide produced by the explosion.

Artillery officers have told me that stories were going the round of the batteries that the Germans fired certain shells at our aeroplanes which, on bursting, set free certain gases which intoxicated the aviators.

A French gunner-major circumstantially related that a German trench which had been heavily shelled with turpinite shells was found full of dead Germans, standing or sitting in life-like attitudes and with faces *quite black*. He said that the look-out man was lying in his natural attitude holding field-glasses to his eyes. He was apparently alive, but was really dead, stiff, and with black face and hands. These statements have not been confirmed, but the stories of similar incidents are many. There is no doubt that lyddite and melinite fumes can, when inhaled, produce sudden poisonous changes. I have myself seen British soldiers and German prisoners, after having been exposed to these fumes, come in with deeply yellow jaundiced skin. One man, in fact, looked exactly like a man suffering from acute jaundice.

It is also said that the fumes induce drowsiness. Turpinite shells were employed at one stage of the war and are to be employed again. M. Turpin has recently been at the front with a French battery. Certainly turpinite does emit dangerous fumes. Many believe that it is some form of cyanogen gas—allied to prussic acid.

The force of these high explosives is well illustrated by an occurrence of 25th January. Previous to making an assault the Germans fired a mine under our front trench near the railway east of Cuinchy. The explosion hurled a piece of rail weighing 25 lbs. a distance of over a mile, into a field close to where some of our men were working.

It is reported that on 1st February the detonation of one of our lyddite shells in the enemy trenches on the embankment south of the canal, threw a German soldier right across the railway and the canal amongst our men on the north side of the latter.

At Fort Condé, on the Aisne, the air concussion of a bursting shell from a French 75 mm. lifted a large four-wheeled country waggon bodily out of a yard and planted it on the roof of a barn. The waggon was not injured. A bursting shell is the very incarnation of violence. Lord Fisher said that "The Essence of War is Violence. Moderation in War is Imbecility. Hit first. Hit hard. Hit everywhere." The big shells to-day do all this.

The fumes emitted by bursting charges of lyddite, melinite, or turpinite must not be confused with the poison gases sent out over our men by the Germans. The lyddite and melinite are put in the shells for a definite object which is permitted by the Hague Convention, and by the opinion of mankind generally.

Their object is to burst the shell at the desired time and distance, and plaster the enemy with the iron or shrapnel. They are not intended to kill, and do not kill by poisonous fumes. The German poison gas is intended to kill, and does produce intolerable agony and lingering deaths, and for this the German stands accused before High Heaven.

NEURASTHENIA OR "NERVES."

Many officers and some men have been sent back from the front in France and Flanders suffering from Nerves. These men are not "nervous" as the public generally understand that term. They are brave and courageous men who are anxious to do their duty. They are, moreover, men who have done their duty in the face of a determined foe, have endured great hardships and discomforts in the trenches and batteries, and have faced death in all the many hellish shapes that it assumes to-day. I said "many officers and some men" have been so afflicted, and it is true that the officer is much more prone to get "nerves" than is the simple soldier. The life of the officer is one of responsibility and worry, but the soldier's mental lot is simpler—he just does what he is told and has "not to reason why." The education and upbringing of the officer are different, as a rule, from that of the soldier, and heredity has an influence on a man's nervous organisation. In civil life anyone can call to mind certain boys and girls who are more "nervous" than others. I do not mean more afraid of danger or more effeminate, but more likely to be exalted or depressed by certain circumstances than their more stolid neighbours. What is true of homes and of schools is equally true of nations. Unreal though it sounds, there is no doubt that the Germans are more emotional than the French, and German leaders know full well the emotional side of their people. The German is easily exalted and can be easily depressed. The Frenchman can be made furiously angry when he is affronted or insulted, but he is not easily depressed, and he is too cautious to be easily exalted. The German soldier and people must be strengthened and mentally sustained by stories of German victories and prowess, but the Frenchman, like the Englishman, is most formidable when he knows the worst there is to know and is "up against things."

It may be that our officers who develop neurasthenia at the front are more emotional and imaginative than those who do not, but they are no less courageous. An officer was sent to England for neurasthenia, and felt ashamed to tell his friends that he was sent back as his "nerve was gone." He was not in the list of wounded, yet his brain and nervous system had received a wound as much as the man with a bullet-hole through his shoulder, and the treatment for these "mental wounds" is like that for most other wounds, "time and rest," but the mental wound also requires quietness. The officer with the mental wound, the nerve shock, the neurasthenia, cannot be treated successfully in the general wards of a noisy hospital. He must be put in quiet and peaceful surroundings and live in an atmosphere free from noise, bustle, and commotion. His treatment must also be directed by physicians who are authorities on this subject. A successful general practitioner or a renowned obstetrician are not likely to achieve brilliant results in treating neurasthenia.

Fortunately the medical profession has already arranged special provision for these nerve cases, and the results, I am sure, will be eminently good.

At Bethune one able artillery officer was brought into the Clearing Hospital suffering from neurasthenia. He had been through the retreat, the fighting on the Marne and Aisne, and at La Bassée, and had done splendid service with his battery, and had been promoted. When I saw him he was walking up and down a room like a caged animal. I wished him good morning, and he pulled up suddenly in his stride, gazed at me with widely open eyes, and replied in a hesitating staccato voice, "G-g-good m-m-morning, doctor." He had never stuttered before. Then away he went up and down again. I got him to sit down on a box and told him to light his pipe and talk about himself. He filled his pipe with difficulty, stuffing the tobacco into the bowl with trembling and agitated fingers. He broke several wooden matches in trying to light them. He had lost the fine, practised discrimination necessary to rub a match on the side of the box, and he "jabbed" his match hard on it. I lit a match and gave it to him, as I was interested to see how he would light the pipe. He let that match fall. I lit another, and with this he burned his finger. I then held a lighted match over his pipe, and in a jerky way he managed to light the tobacco; but he could not smoke properly, and the pipe soon went out. In the same jerky way he told me that he was forty-four years of age and had never been ill before. He was a good rifle shot, and had killed big game in India. He was a fair billiard player, and had been a temperate man all his life in all things. Talking in his spasmodic fashion, he had to stop for a word, and he then waved his hand about and frowned, as if angry with himself for having forgotten it. Up till a week ago he had been in perfect health, although the "strain" of the war had been tremendous; then one of his brother officers and a sergeant had been killed close beside him, and his guns had to be moved to another position under a heavy fire. He could not sleep that night, and the firing of the guns, which previously had not troubled him in the least, now worried him. Next day he could not eat. In a few days he was a physical and mental wreck. He was sent to England, and I heard that he had made a complete recovery.

One officer developed neurasthenia on the Aisne. His regiment had done brilliantly, but had suffered severe losses. The officer said that he was going to blow his brains out, so he was invalided into the hands of the doctors and later made a good recovery. He was suffering from the effects of strain and mental shock.

Another officer on the staff was standing close by his

chief when a shell fell near, killing his chief outright. The staff officer had to be sent home for neurasthenia.

Our wounded often show signs of neurasthenia. I well remember at the hospital at Bethune one man who had had to have his arm off at the shoulder joint for a bad shrapnel wound. He was dangerously ill and semi-conscious for several days. When he had fully roused to his surroundings and the knowledge of his weakness he was like a little child, crying and begging me to get him away from the sound of the firing. He said that he would be happy if only he could get away to some place where he would not hear the sound of the guns. On the day the German aeroplane dropped a bomb near the hospital the windows of the building shook and rattled with the concussion, and this poor devil screamed aloud with terror and tried to get out of bed and crawl away—anywhere from the sound of the firing.

The French nursing sisters told me that the wounded Frenchmen work themselves into a terrible state of excitement in hospital when the firing is very brisk. They beg and beg to be taken away to the south of France, as far away as possible from the sound of conflict.

These were all brave men with injured nervous systems.

SMALL ARM AMMUNITION.

The Germans have charged the British, French, Russians, and Belgians with using Dum-Dum bullets. The Austrians have made the same charge against the

Serbians and Montenegrins. The Triple Entente and its Allies have accused the Germans and Austrians of firing Dum-Dum bullets—so there you are.

The Dum-Dum bullet was first made at Dum-Dum, near Calcutta. It was a Lee-Enfield bullet with an imperfect nickel sheath. This nickel or cupro-nickel sheath in the Dum-Dum stops at the "shoulder" of the bullet, and the point is therefore bare lead, a continuation of the core of the bullet. Some modifications of the Dum-Dum exist. By rubbing the point of a nickel-coated Lee-Enfield bullet on a rough stone the cover is rubbed off, exposing the core of lead. A saw or file can make incisions in the long axis of the bullet exposing the lead this way, but leaving the tip covered with nickel. The destiny of a Dum-Dum is to break up when it strikes a bone. If it strikes a bone at a high rate of velocity it fragments and rips and tears the bone and surrounding soft structures. It is supposed to have greater "stopping power" against an infantry charge than an undeformed bullet. This supposition is incorrect. Certainly a Dum-Dum in traversing a limb or the chest can cause terrible and widespread destruction. In wounds inflicted by a Dum-Dum bits of the lead core and casing are scattered in various directions. But,—and this is important,—the same thing can be found in a wound inflicted by an undeformed Lee-Metford, Lebel, or Mauser bullet. The only certain proof of the employment of the Dum-Dums is to find them in the trenches captured from the enemy, or in the cartridge belts of wounded or prisoners. Again, a man may have a bullet wound with a small entrance hole and a large, gaping, jagged exit. One unaccustomed to bullet wounds would immediately say that such a wound was caused by an explosive bullet. But it can be caused by the ordinary Lee-Metford, Lebel, and Mauser bullets. I have seen these wounds frequently amongst Germans, French, and British. The explanation is that the bullet on striking a bone often carries along with it a fragment, large or small, and it is this fragment of bone that tears out a passage to the exit wound. The German bullet is easily extracted from the cartridge. It is almost impossible to extract the Lee-Metford bullet without strong instruments. The Germans have made use of this fact to extract the bullet from the cartridge and put it back "upside down," that is, with the nickel point inside the metal cartridge case, and the base with its exposed lead core outwards. Such a bullet on striking a bone expands and fragments, and causes great damage. I am not repeating a rumour when I make this statement. I have seen these cartridges with the inverted bullets in the belts of German prisoners captured in the trenches. Other surgeons have seen them also. The French say that it is a common practice amongst the Germans, and so did our men at Ypres. One German prisoner on the Yser when confronted with these bullets taken from his own belt, admitted having used them. He said that his company officer told him that they were useful to break down barbed-wire entanglements!

There is one interesting point about the German bullet, and that is its property of spinning on its short axis when it strikes an object. The centre of gravity of the German bullet is low down on its base, owing to its long and tapering shoulder. It therefore turns over on reaching its object. I had on the Aisne one man of the Norfolk Regiment admitted with a tiny entrance wound between the great and second toes of the foot. The bullet was found lodged in the large heel bone, and its base was facing towards the entrance wound. It could not have entered the foot in that position, because the entrance wound was too small. A bullet spinning round when traversing a limb can cause considerably more damage than one that pursues a direct course, and this fact is important in brain injuries. The bullet penetrates the skull by a small punctured opening, and then whirls round and round inside the brain. It may then again strike the bone on the other side with its long axis and cause considerable shattering and bleeding. This spinning action of the Mauser was a thing that every surgeon had to remember when treating his wounded.

The Hague Convention of 1907 prohibits "the use of projectiles calculated to cause unnecessary suffering." The Hague Declarations of 1899 decide to "abstain from the use of bullets which expand or flatten easily in the human body," such as bullets with a hard envelope which does not entirely cover the core or is pierced with incisions. The St. Petersburg Declaration of 1868 agrees to abolish the use of "any projectile of a weight below 400 grams which is either explosive or charged with fulminating or inflammable substances."

The *British Medical Journal* of 21st November 1914 reports as follows on the subject of small arm ammunition:

The British service ammunition is known technically as Mark VII. ·303 S.A. Ammunition. The length of the bullet is 1·28 inches; weight, 174 grains; muzzle velocity, 2440 feet per second. The bullet is a pointed one with an envelope of cupro-nickel which completely covers the core except at the base. The ordinary German service ammunition is very similar. Length of bullet, 1·105 inches; weight, 154 grains; muzzle velocity, 2970 feet per second. This bullet is pointed, with a steel envelope coated with cupro-nickel covering the cone except at the base. Both bullets carry out the provisions of the Hague Convention.

There is clear evidence that Germany has not confined herself solely to this unobjectionable ammunition. Her troops, both in Togoland and in France, have been proved to have used bullets with a soft core and hard, thin envelope not entirely covering the core, which type of bullet is expanding and therefore expressly prohibited by the Hague Convention.

Such bullets, of no less than three types, were found on the bodies of dead native soldiers serving with the German armed forces against British troops in Togoland in August, and on the persons of German, European, and native armed troops captured by us in that colony. All the British wounded treated in the British hospitals during the operations in Togoland were wounded by soft-nosed bullets of large calibre, and the injuries which these projectiles inflicted, in marked contrast to those treated by the British medical staff amongst the German wounded, were extremely severe, bones being shattered and the tissue so extensively damaged that amputation had to be performed. The use of these bullets was the subject of a written protest by the general officer commanding the British troops in Nigeria to the German acting governor of Togoland.

Again at Gundelu, in France, on 19th September 1914, soft-nosed bullets were found on the dead bodies of German soldiers of the Landwehr, and on the persons of soldiers of the Landwehr made prisoners of war by the British troops. One of these bullets has reached the War Office. It is undoubtedly expanding and directly prohibited by the Hague Convention. I am sure that Germany will be terribly upset at this, for Germany, we know, pays great respect to the articles of the Hague Convention!

CHAPTER XVII.

WE LEAVE BETHUNE.

One afternoon a German aeroplane dropped a bomb at the hospital gate, and a second one on a house near the gate. They burst with a terrific crash, shook the building and rattled the glass and startled us all. The same voyaging Taube dropped another bomb in the square of the city, and an old woman, a man, and a baby were struck. The old lady had to have her leg amputated and died on the succeeding day; the man received a shell wound in the back of the head and he died a few days afterwards; the baby was injured in the stomach and also died next day. One of our Army Service Corps men was struck by a piece of shell on the leg and received a serious wound. A corporal of the Army Service ran upstairs to me in the ward where I was busy dressing some cases and excitedly told me that his back was broken and that he thought he would soon be paralysed. We undressed him and found that a small piece of shell had made a slight wound on the muscles of the back, but that he was otherwise all right. He was reassured about the paralysis and the broken back. Two days afterwards another German aeroplane —or it may have been the same beast that had visited us before—flew over the city and dropped some more bombs, killing some unfortunate people and injuring others.

On the following morning at three o'clock I was in one of the wards admitting some wounded men just in from the trenches, when the unmistakable burst of a Black Maria was heard close at hand. The shell had burst not far from the hospital, and was followed by two more, one near the railway station, and one near the college not far away. The Germans had the range perfectly, and we expected a big bombardment. The authorities decided that Bethune was no longer a safe place for our Clearing Hospitals, and we were ordered to prepare for the evacuation of our wounded as soon as possible. This was soon done, and all were conveyed by ambulance motors to the hospital trains, with the exception of seven men. These men were all dying from severe injuries to the brain, and no good would be served by sending them down to the Base. So the seven poor fellows were put in beds alongside each other in one ward, and in three days they were dead, and buried in the now well-filled cemetery at Bethune.

The two Clearing Hospitals in the city—British and Indian—were sent to Chocques, near Lillers.

It was with a little heartache that I left Bethune and its good sisters. We had passed through days and nights of racking work and worry, and we had the satisfaction of feeling that we had all done our best. It is mournful to leave a place associated with many stirring episodes and with many warm friendships, for in times like those at Bethune firm friendships were quickly made. In saying good-bye one seems to leave them behind for ever—and that is always sad.

The nuns at this hospital were simply splendid all through, and I can quite understand how the religious sisters have come to their own again in France.

From the earliest times and up till about eight years ago all the nursing in the French hospitals was done by sisters belonging to the various religious orders. Then came one of the big political upheavals for which France has been so noted in the past, and the nursing sisters gradually disappeared from the hospitals owing to the hostility of the State to the Church and all connected with it. The nursing sisters of these orders were at the time of this change well-trained medical and surgical nurses. As they were no longer able to exercise their professional skill, and no more of the younger nuns were trained in nursing, it followed that on the outbreak of war only the older nuns were capable of undertaking skilled nursing in the many hospitals. The demand for nurses was a clamant one, for from the very beginning of the war there were large casualties. It was said that the nursing by the lay sisters who succeeded the religious sisters was not of such a high order as in the old days owing to the absence of the strict and rigid discipline, the very fibre of the life of a sister in religion. I have heard this both from French surgeons and from visiting British surgeons.

When the war broke out France was as ill prepared

in her military medical branch as we were, and she was suddenly confronted with the problem of handling and treating many thousands of wounded.

M. Clemenceau, an ex-Premier of France and a Doctor of Medicine, is also the editor of *L'Homme Enchaîné*. At the outbreak of war this journal was known as *L'Homme Libre*, and Clemenceau so violently attacked the medical disorganisation and lack of preparation that the paper was promptly suppressed. It, however, emerged next day under its new title, *The Man in Chains*, and under this title appears daily in Paris.

Clemenceau's efforts, however, were continued, and France soon had everything in good going order. It was at this critical phase that the Franciscan sisters, and the sisters of other religious orders, quietly took their places beside the wounded French soldiers. Just as quietly they opened up their convents, churches, and buildings, warehouses, châteaux, cottages, railway waiting-rooms, and turned them into hospitals for the wounded and sick men. Working tirelessly night and day, knowing no fatigue and shrinking from no task or danger, and glorying in their mission, they performed marvels. The younger sisters were put to subordinate nursing duties, and so rigorously trained by the elder ones in the principles of nursing.

These juniors are now very competent nurses, for they learn quickly amongst the ample material that war provides. The wounded French soldier loves and idolises the nursing sister. He demands her presence, and makes her his confidante. The nun is supremely happy to be back in her old place, and pets and humours the wounded soldier, soothes his ardent soul, and, by her skill, heals his wounds.

I do not think that any future government of France will ever dare to oust the religious sisters from the hospitals. These quiet-voiced, simple-robed women, carrying help and compassionate pity in the welter of blood and slaughter, have come " to their own " again.

When writing of the religious orders one naturally thinks of the priests of France, and one of the many interesting and instructive evolutions taking place during this war is that of the changing relation of the people and State towards the Catholic Church.

One has only to be a little time with the French troops in the field to recognise and be impressed by their deep attachment to the Catholic Church. I visited many churches in France and Belgium during the earlier stages of the war, and at all hours, and have always found, sometimes few, sometimes many, Belgian and French soldiers on their knees and devoutly at prayer in the sacred buildings. Women, of course, were always to be seen there, but that was not surprising. It was surprising to see so many soldiers.

The French soldier takes his religion seriously in these days, and is not ashamed, whenever the opportunity occurs, to enter a church and pray. It was rare to see a khaki soldier praying in church; one often saw them there on visits of curiosity gazing at the old windows and old scroll-work of the churches. The

British soldier will always attend a church parade, and he will be most reverent during a service, and will sing lustily and amen loudly; but a church parade is to him very often a drill, and Tommy cheerfully attends a drill parade because it is his duty to. In reading letters from British soldiers at the front and comparing them with those of French soldiers one cannot help being struck by the religious serious note pervading those of the latter, and its absence in the former. It may be that we are less emotional than the French, and as a nation are shy of writing of our inner selves. It was my duty once to censor the letters written by wounded men in a Clearing Hospital at the front. The letters were distinctly humorous at times; only two discussed matters of faith. In one a soldier was writing to his mother, and he said, "I pray every day as I promised you to. I pray standing up, and always time my prayer for three o'clock in the afternoon, for that is the time when the fellows over the way let off most of their big guns and rifles at us." This man was either a wag and teasing his mother, or he really believed in the efficacy of surrounding himself with an atmosphere of prayer when the enemy fire was hottest. The other fervent letter was from a soldier who had received a slight shell wound of the scalp. His was a letter written to a clergyman near London. This warrior informed the clergyman that he prayed silently amongst his comrades, and daily read a passage out of his Testament. The letter ended up by asking the clergyman to send him some Woodbine cigarettes, as he, the writer, hadn't had a smoke for a fortnight and saw no chance of getting one. I showed this letter to our field chaplain, who visited this Christian soldier in the ward. The chaplain told me afterwards that the man was absolutely destitute of any religious beliefs, and had never read a Testament in his life; and furthermore—that he had three packets of Woodbine cigarettes, and had also smoked a considerable number during the past fortnight.

French officers have told me that before the war it was considered bad form for a military officer to attend Mass, and that an officer who attended Mass regularly need not expect promotion in the Army. Attending Mass is not considered bad form to-day, and soldiers of all grades from general to grenadier attend the services in the field. Was the religious trait there all the time, and only held back by the conventional strictness, or has the seriousness of the war compelled a little self-analysis and a return to the faith of their fathers? My impression is that the priests and the nursing sisters of the religious orders have helped to stir up this present state amongst a people who have always been, deep down, much attached to their Church and its religious observances. Even the Reign of Terror could not stamp out the influence of the Church in France, although it turned churches into meat marts and blacksmiths' forges, and plastered their walls with "Liberté, Egalité, Fraternité." The French priest has no official status in the State. He is simply a citizen, and is liable, like all other citizens, to be mobilised for military duty. Over 20,000 French priests and brothers of various orders are serving with the French colours in this war. I have spoken to French priests about this law that compels them to serve as soldiers. They do not cavil at it, and, in fact, prefer to act the patriot's part, for the priest is every bit a good Frenchman. Be the priest a simple soldier in the trenches, with battery, commissariat, ammunition, or brancardiers, he is nevertheless still a priest, and is at all times ready and eager to exercise his priestly duties. He has proved himself time and time again to be a cool, intrepid, and reliable soldier, and he has also proved himself in the hour of trial a comfort and spiritual help to those about to die. One has heard of hundreds of instances in this war when the priest, serving as soldier in the ranks, has conducted Mass in some broken-down cottage or barn in the firing zone, buried his dead comrades with the rites of the Church, and carried out the last offices to the dying. One of the ablest of the French artillery officers, now in charge of a battery, is a priest, and in times of peace is a well-known Abbé and writer on theology. Another learned Abbé and a great preacher was mobilised in July, and was badly wounded at Charleroi. When lying stricken on the ground he heard a mortally wounded soldier calling him. The Abbé painfully crawled to the dying soldier and administered the last office, and while doing so was again wounded. He was later on conveyed by hospital train to Paris. President Poincaré had heard the story, and met the train on its arrival in Paris. He went into the carriage where lay the badly wounded and apparently dying Abbé, and decorated him with the Legion d'Honneur. I am glad to say that the Abbé, although now a cripple, recovered from his wounds.

The Aumonier to the French Hospital at Bethune was a very fine priest. He was not mobilised as a soldier owing to defective vision, but he acted as priest and as a stretcher-bearer to the hospital. His life-long friend, another priest and lecturer on Natural History at the College at Bethune, was fighting as a private in the Argonne. One day the Abbé told me that he had received a letter from his friend describing his life in the trenches, saying, " I live the life of a rabbit. I live in a hole in the ground. At night I come out to feed."

A few days after this the Abbé heard that his friend was killed—shot dead through the head. When the Abbé told me of this I murmured the usual, " Hard luck."

" No," said the Abbé, becoming very serious. " It is not what you call the Hard Luck. It is the good luck. It is how a good priest would wish to die."

It has been asked many times during this war, " What is Christianity doing after the past 1900 years ?" and many have answered, " Crucified men and women. Mutilitated prisoners of war. Outraged women and slaughtered children. Cities and towns in ashes. Misery, tears, and the moaning of millions." If this is the indictment, it is not against Christianity, but against one people only, that of Lutheran Germany.

But these hellish deeds of "Christian" Germany have but served to bring more clearly and brightly into view the Christian spirit of other peoples' brotherliness, help for the distressed, and that

> "Kindness in another's trouble,
> Courage in your own."

The Belgian and French soldiers fighting at first to defend their homes, their women, and their children and old men, and fighting now for vengeance to punish the bloody invaders, are examples of a good, healthy Christianity.

The open, warm welcome of France and England to the Belgian refugees, the colossal funds for the alleviation of distress, and helping of the wounded and the sick, show that the "greatest of these," Charity, is not yet dead on the earth.

Our definition of "Christianity" depends upon the point of view. To me the Turco and the Gurkha are very good Christians and the German nation is infidel. Every General Order issued by the Kaiser ends not with an appeal to the Almighty, but with an affirmation that God is fighting for the German cause.

The Saxons and Bavarians will sack a town and inflict nameless horrors on helpless civilians, shoot old men for sport, kill children, torture women, commit sacrilege in the churches, smash altars and relics, destroy historic and beautiful windows and treasures of art, bayonet priests, violate shrieking nuns, and with hands smeared in blood they will at the word of command praise their German God.

CHAPTER XVIII.

OVER THE BELGIAN FRONTIER.

OUR Clearing Hospital remained at Chocques for four or five days, and while here had a fair, but not a large, number of wounded. These were quickly sent off by hospital trains, which pulled on to a siding not far from us. The Indian Clearing Hospital was now also establishing itself in the small town, and the Indian hospital assistants were a source of great and wondering curiosity to the small boys and girls. Our Clearing Hospital was now ordered to a place farther north, and as I had only been temporarily attached to it during a time of great rush at Bethune, my place was now with my own Field Ambulance at the front, and somewhere near the Belgian frontier.

A motor-car going to Hazebrouck gave me a lift as far as there, and another driver brought me to Bailleul. Here, after I had reported my arrival, Surgeon-General Porter informed me of the exact location of my ambulance.

Bailleul is a town of considerable importance in the north of France, and has been the object of many visits from Taubes, a sure indication that there must be a church or a hospital in Bailleul. The church and the hospital were very close together, and the Taubes made many a gallant attempt to get them both. One evening one of them got the hospital—a bomb fell fair on the roof and into a ward full of wounded men, killing two and wounding again a man already grievously wounded. The old church has so far escaped. The square at Bailleul near the church was a busy place in those days, as the town was a Divisional Headquarters and a corps "poste commandement," and where there are headquarters and "brass hats" there also are many rank and file. It was here that, some weeks later, I saw that fine battalion, the Liverpool Scottish, parade in the street and march out to the trenches. They were standing on parade in the street for about twenty minutes before moving off and the day was bitterly cold. The bare knees of the men looked blue and the kilt did not impress us as a good winter dress. Why Highlanders choose to expose their knees is quite beyond me. The knee joint is a big and complex anatomical structure, and is easily affected by sudden changes of temperature, so why cover up every other joint in the body and leave this bare?

Greatly daring though the ladies are to-day in their draping arrangements, they do not dare to walk about with bare knees. What prevents them must certainly be their appreciation of the delicacy of this joint—the delicate mechanism of an important articulation.

Twenty years hence, veterans of the Liverpool Scottish will tell their children how they got rheumatism in their knee joints from the cold mud of the Flanders trenches in the year of our Lord 1914.

I left Bailleul on a Red-Cross Wolseley car driven by a queer character who used to be with us on the Aisne doing transport work. He was thought to have been killed and duly buried, and I was therefore agreeably surprised to see my odd friend again. He was a wonderfully cheery pessimist. He usually had a long budget of most depressing news, of disasters by flood and field, and great disappointments, but he envisaged them all with a rosy hue and predicted a great to-morrow. He did not like the war, for although it had not changed his occupation—that of a chauffeur—it had seriously affected his emoluments. In the piping times of peace he would take small parties on touring journeys in France, Germany, and Switzerland—sometimes a honeymoon couple, sometimes an American millionaire, and he did exceedingly well in tips.

We had a rough passage up from Bailleul and were twice bogged in the mud beside the road, and had twice to be hauled out. The roads here, and right over the frontier into southern Belgium, were very bad in these days. Our men, when on the Aisne, said many hard words about the mud there, but the Aisne was an asphalt path compared with Belgium.

However, we slowly squelched and skidded our way over the Belgian frontier and reached Ouderdom, not very far from Ypres. For the last few miles we had been following Napoleon's maxim to his Marshals: "Marching on the sound of the guns." The heavy artillery, French, British, and German, was making a deafening roar.

This really completed the journey from the Aisne to Flanders. We were at our "farthest north," and this journey impressed one with the length of the huge battle-line, although it only embraced, after all, a part of the great whole. From Switzerland to the Channel stretched a wavy line of trenches, across plains, spanning canals, through and around swamps, in front of great cities and small villages, traversing great forests and over mountain passes and peaks. At one end submerged country flooded by Alpine snow, sand dunes at the other; and in these trenches lined with soldiers, and swept by artillery, stern fighting was going on over practically every mile.

Our ambulance headquarters was about the most God-forsaken place that one could possibly imagine. The first impression one received was a dirty pond, full of fetid water and surrounded by heaped-up straw manure. The Belgian, like the Frenchman, loves to have a manure heap at his front door. Closely abutting on this putrefactive manure was the cottage itself, with one front room, a small side-room or box off this front room, a kitchen, a bedroom, and another box at the back. From the kitchen a rickety stair led up to a windy loft full of corn and hops and bags of potatoes.

Next the living quarters and part of the house came stalls for cattle, and the *tout ensemble* was unlovely and smelly. Twelve medical officers, two chaplains, and a quartermaster lived in the tiny little front room, or crowded round a table in it. When the table was in the room there was barely space to pass between it and the wall. Six or seven officers slept on the floor of this den at night, and in the morning had to rise early, roll up their valises and pack them round the wall. The O.C. and a chaplain slept in the box off our only room, and the rest of us slept in the loft amidst the wheat and hops and the bitter cold draughts.

Our cooks lived, smoked, worked, and slept in the kitchen, and this apartment Madame invaded during the day to do her domestic cooking. Madame "with the terrible voice" gave our cooks a bad time, and frequently chased them out and took their pots and pans off the fire, utterly disorganising our meals.

Madame was not popular, and in my dreams I sometimes still hear her raucous voice.

The Flemish farmer, the proud owner of this very dirty and uninviting farm, had a family of three little children, and was besides the humble husband of the lady whose voice was more terrifying than the screech of bursting shrapnel.

Poor Madame, she did not look kindly on us, and we never even saw her smile—except once, and that story comes later.

At 4 a.m. her strident, penetrating tones would fill the cottage and wake us all to a world of cold and discomfort, of greasy bacon, muddy tea, and sodden mousy bread.

She was watchful and suspicious of our men, who slept with the poultry in the surrounding stables and out-houses, and openly accused them of stealing her straw.

What they could do with the straw after having stolen it Madame did not choose to say—perhaps she thought that they ate it!

We met many Flemish besides Madame and her family at this time, and although we sympathised greatly with them, we could not bring ourselves to like them. It was all so different with the French, whom we liked and who liked us. The Flemings did not seem to care for us; they certainly never made us any demonstrations of affection. Perhaps it was the difference in tongue. They spoke French with an Irish-Dutch brogue, and our accent was, of course, a pure Anglo-Parisian.

French officers told us here that they did not like the Flemings, and that the Flemings were not cordial with them. Belgian officers, it is well known, do not see eye to eye with the French officers, but pull amazingly well with the British, to whom they are warm and communicative.

Tommy Atkins as a rule likes every one, but he neither understood nor cared for the Flemings. This was quite noticeable. We found those round Ouderdom, Ypres, and Dickebusch sullen, dour, and suspicious. We were not welcomed, and their surly, heavy manner towards us was very apparent. There was no responsiveness, no *gaieté de cœur*, no cheerfulness.

Historical traditions and the likes and hates of centuries die hard. The Flemings and the English had often been friends in the past, but the French and Flemings had always been on opposite sides of the fence, and whenever the French came into the Flemish garden it was to fight, and not to play.

We wondered if Madame of our cottage knew her Belgian history. We were quite sure that she would have been more amiable and sweet had she known that Flanders had been England's ally in the Hundred Years' War, and that the bowmen of Mons were more than once ranged on England's side; that Baldwin II., Count of Flanders, a former ruler of the land where stood Madame's farm, was a son-in-law of Alfred the Great of England, and that Baldwin V., also a Count of Flanders, was father-in-law to William the Conqueror, and fitted out Flemish ships to convey Flemish men to Pevensey to kill Harold's Anglo-Saxons.

The Flemings have long memories about the French, and never forget the "Battle of the Spurs" or the "Battle of Roosebeke," for in these two epoch-making battles the French were the enemy.

The manifesto issued by the King of the Belgians to his people at the beginning of the war in August cited the Battle of the Spurs fought at Courtrai. At this famous encounter, a band of Flemish artisans and citizens, armed with billhooks, axes, and scythes, attacked with the maddest fury a disciplined French army of steel-clad knights and men-at-arms and utterly defeated it. This battle reference was hardly quite happy when Joffre was hurrying his Army Corps over the frontier to Namur.

At Roosebeke, in 1382, the French met another citizen army under Philip van Artevelde, and slew him and twenty-five thousand men. It is said that Flemish fathers and mothers handed down this bitter tale to their children for three centuries, and in later years told of Cassel, Ramillies, Oudenarde, Malplaquet, Jemappes, and Waterloo—all glaring instances of French turbulence on peaceful Flanders land. So the Flemings were distrustful always of the Gallic cock, and had apparently forgotten about their connection with our Alfred the Great and our William of Normandy.

During our occupation of this mean farmhouse, situated behind its Flemish manure heap, the weather was bitingly cold. The rain of the first week was succeeded by a heavy snow and frost, and as we had no fire of any sort and were not able to take much physical exercise, we were all day and night chilled to our very marrow.

November 1914 in Flanders will be remembered by many thousands of Englishmen as a month of intense and bitter cold, when to the dangers and ever-present death of the trenches were added the miseries and tortures of frostbitten feet and legs, and a merciless cutting wind. This was the period when men, stiffened and paralysed with cold, had to be pulled out of the trenches and dragged or carried to the rear to bring back a slowing circulation to the affected limbs. This was also the period when men could not be spared from the firing line, when the Germans were making those formidable rushes in strong columns, and leaving thousands of dead to mark the place where the rush had been stayed and the column crumpled up.

The little town of Dickebusch was on the road to our left, and through it ran a highway to Ypres. Where the road turned to the right into Ypres was an advanced station of a Field Ambulance, and, as one of the medical officers of it was known to me, I walked along this highway one morning in order to hear the latest news. He was always a very safe man to call upon for news, for what he did not know authentically, he would invent. The road to this advanced station lay behind several batteries of French "seventy-fives," the pride and glory of the French gunner. The road was quite close to these guns, but they were so wonderfully concealed with straw and branches of trees that an ordinary traveller would have passed them by until their presence was indicated by their mighty roar. The gunners were hard at it this morning, pouring an unending string of bursting shells on the German positions, and the din was terrible.

Suddenly the Germans got the range of the road. One shell burst far in front of me on the road, and one far behind about the same moment, and a bolt for cover was the immediate sequence. I got into a dug-out behind some French guns and then witnessed a wonderful display of artillery practice. Shell after shell fell with marvellous precision up and down the road, and one followed the other with a lightning speed. The road was excavated with volcanic craters, of flying stones and earth clouds, and mighty showers of *débris* were sprayed tumultuously on every side. A French officer pointed out where the next shell would land; and he was always right—he knew the "general idea" possessing the mind of the German gunner, and correctly surmised that after the road had been systematically covered, the firing would cease. It was a big waste of ammunition, for nothing was damaged except the road, and the French gunners, as soon as the firing was over, ran to their pet "seventy-fives" and opened furiously back in order to show that their bark was as good as ever. The French batteries at this particular place did enormous damage to the Germans in their attacks south of Ypres, and as they are no longer at this roadside but somewhere farther on, no valuable information is being given away in relating the fact.

The French gunners, both at this critical phase of the war and on the Aisne, were wonderful fellows. Night and day, in rain, hail, sleet, or snow, their great guns never stopped. In the blackest night and in howling gales of sleety wind they could be heard near by and in the far distance, for ever pounding into the enemy. This policy of continuous fire is wonderfully heartening to the French troops in the trenches, and the moral effect is tremendous. On the Aisne the French guns were always busy, but the British, alas, were generally silent. I have heard men on the Aisne pathetically say, "Why don't our guns fire?" "Why don't they reply to the German fire?" and the questioning was not confined to soldiers, for it was a common topic of conversation amongst officers. On the Aisne we did not have enough artillery, and we had not enough ammunition for the artillery we did have. It was the same at this period at Ypres. England, the greatest engineering country of the world, the richest and most prosperous Empire of this or any other time, made a very poor showing on the Continent. Small as our army was, it was not equipped perfectly. Our army in France may have been the " best shooting army," but if so it was with the rifle. In artillery we were entirely outclassed by the Germans and put to eternal shame by the French. On the Aisne the Germans had big 8-inch howitzers and we had nothing to meet them. Against the guns that had battered the forts of Maubeuge and crumpled up Namur what had we to offer? Nothing. The Germans had an unlimited supply of machine-guns on the Aisne and the Yser, and we had a paltry few. We were short of ammunition, but the Germans and the French had plenty.

When we required high explosive shells to beat down entrenchments and trenches we had nothing but shrapnel, which was absolutely useless for this purpose. Because shrapnel was effective in the South African War and high explosives unnecessary there, it was concluded that the same set of circumstances would be repeated in France and Belgium.

In September 1914 I saw the four 6-inch howitzer batteries arrive on the Aisne from England, and the news of their arrival spread like wildfire amongst our men, who thought that at last " mighty England was sending mighty guns." They were mighty guns right enough, but there was not enough ammunition sent with them. As a nation we always muddle through, but it is rather pitiful to think that muddles mean the death of many brave men, and that our woeful lack of big guns and ammunition has meant many British graves in France and Flanders.

A ride through Ypres at this time was an interesting and exciting affair — interesting from the historic associations of the old Flemish capital, and exciting from the German " Black Marias " falling about. The old Cloth Hall was then still standing—only one corner and a door had been battered about, but Ypres itself was very mournful and desolate. A bombarded town, empty of all its people and with ruins all round where once was industry, wealth, and moving crowds, presents a very sad spectacle. I suppose Ypres, stormy as her history has been in the past, had never been so empty before. At one time 200,000 people were said to have lived in Ypres. That was in the days of her splendour as the ancient capital of Flanders, when the wonderful Cloth Hall was built by the cloth-workers of the thirteenth century, in that turbulent epoch when citizens and workpeople were fighting down and curbing the old feudal tyranny—for it was in Belgium that the common people established the first free city north of the Alps.

On the ride through this famous old city to our positions beyond, the terrible evidences of the German bombardment surrounded one in monumental impressiveness. Dead horses were lying in coagulated pools of blood in every street. Whole rows of old, closely-built Spanish and Flemish houses and shops were crumbled and shattered. The *pavé* was ripped, torn, and covered with window glass shattered into millions of fine fragments; roofs had disappeared from some houses, and walls blown out of others. Tumbled masonry, smoking ashes, and excavated, torn-up roadways—all bore witness to the terrible character of the first German bombardment.

In one tobacconist's shop in the square, just opposite the Cloth Hall, the large plate-glass window had been completely destroyed, but the shop stood otherwise uninjured and intact. One could easily have taken boxes of cigars and pipes by simply putting a hand through the window-frame in passing, but although the temptation was there, not one cigar was touched by a British soldier. Imagine the genial Saxon or the crucifying Bavarian letting such a chance slip!

I got off my horse and led it through the street, as it clearly did not like passing the dead horses on the roadway. After having tied it to a street-post in front of a fair-sized hotel or *estaminet*, I walked into the front bar-parlour, which was open to the street. The evidences of a hasty exit were ludicrously patent. A half-emptied glass of beer and a full one stood close together on the bar counter, and near them lay a good pipe full of tobacco which had not been lighted. On a small table in a corner of the café was a tray with two large empty clean glasses; on the same table stood a bottle of red wine, and close beside it a corkscrew, holding the impaled extracted cork. One light chair near this table lay overturned on the floor; the other had been hastily drawn back, as was shown by the tracks on the sawdust floor. I thought of Pompeii when old Vesuvius belched ashes and molten lava and buried the gay Roman pleasure-city as it stood. The Pompeian wine-bibbers and "mine host" could not escape from that engulfing darkness and the fiery cinders, and perforce died nobly standing by their bottles. But in that drinking-room at Ypres there was no dying the death beside the beer and the good red wine. No Sherlock Holmes was necessary to reconstruct the picture—the two cronies drinking their morning ale at the bar, and the two comfortable Yprian burghers waiting for the filling of their glasses from the bottle just uncorked, the burly "mine host" in white apron and with bottle in hand—all suddenly electrified by a sinister whistling overhead, and then the mighty explosion, the roar of falling masonry, the smashing of hundreds of window-panes, the concussion of air; then another earthquake smash, and then another, till the house and street were rocking with the shocks. This was no time to light a pipe, to drink amber beer and ruddy wine. It was time to get out of Ypres. So down went the forgotten pipe and bottle, back went the chairs, and out streamed our terrified quintet to the tormented street, leaving the room and its contents as I saw it.

On approaching the bridge on the far side of the

town I saw the only remaining inhabitant. This was a middle-aged woman with a grey shawl over her head and shoulders, and she was looking out of a window of a partly shattered house. I felt sorry for her, she looked so very lonely in that broken house.

That afternoon she was arrested by the Belgians as a spy. My compassion had been utterly thrown away.

Near this same bridge on another occasion my arrival was providential. An Army Service Corps driver was speeding his motor towards the city when he was struck by enemy shrapnel. He had just sufficient strength to stop his lorry before fainting from the shock and the rush of blood from a grievous wound of the right thigh. Blood was pumping out of the wound, and it appeared as if the femoral artery had been torn. Fortunately it was not, and we were soon able to control the hæmorrhage, put the wounded man on his lorry, and drive him back to one of the ambulance stations in a cottage near the roadside.

The road from Ypres to our trenches was a busy but pathetic highway—busy with marching men, waggons, gallopers, generals, and staff officers, and pathetic from the many graves and small graveyards near the roadside and the many full ambulance waggons rumbling along on the uneven, jolty *pavé*.

The road was frequently visited with enemy shells, and no one travelled along it unless on business. "Trespassers will be prosecuted" was an unnecessary injunction on the Ypres roads.

The headquarter staff of the 15th Brigade beyond Ypres had a narrow escape one morning. A big shell burst in the grounds of the château occupied by the Brigadier and his staff. The staff, who were in the building at the time, went out to look at the hole it had made. Whilst looking at the pit, another shell landed on the château itself and burst into the room just vacated by them. A soldier servant was killed and one staff officer was wounded.

An advanced ambulance station, with wounded men and medical officers in it, was struck fairly by another shell and badly holed, causing loss of life. No place was safe from these long bowls of the enemy, and though artillery practice of this sort may not be of much military importance, it yet produces an air of uncertainty and caution and jumpiness.

The country surrounding Ypres and Ypres itself were very dismal. The old elm trees on the roads, and the silent, deserted streets were shrouded in a ghostly veil of melancholy.

On a subsequent visit to the site of the old Cloth Hall one saw little more than ruins, for the famous building had in the interval been correctly ranged by the enemy guns and duly shattered. Later on more destruction took place, and visitors of the year 2015 will be shown some stones and broken pillars, all that was left of a famous hall which had stood for seven centuries and had been destroyed " one hundred years ago."

When peace comes again to Belgium, Ypres and its roads, its Hill 60 and its graves will be a place of holy pilgrimage to thousands of English, French, and Germans, for here fell and are buried their bravest dead.

But the curious tripper and the Cook's tourist had better keep away from Ypres. Let the friends of the dead and the quiet country folk have the land in their possession for a season.

The railway station at Vlamertinge, near Ypres, frequently had a very fine armoured train in its sidings. The train was manned by Jack Tars with naval guns, and the engine and car looked very attractive in a wonderful coat of futurist colours—splashes of green and khaki and brown. This *H.M.S Chameleon* was a very good cruiser and very nippy in moving across country. The sailors were very cheerful and seemed to like their ship amazingly.

On the roads near our headquarters running from Renninghelst to Vlamertinge, and hence along the main highway to Ypres, a large number of Belgian soldiers were at work repairing the *pavé* and widening the road surface by laying prepared trunks of trees laid closely together in the mud at the sides. They were fine sturdy men and full of life and cheerfulness, a different type altogether from the countryfolk we met in the farms. These were the men who had fought from Liége to the Yser, and were still on Belgian soil. They were very bitter about the Germans. They said that they asked for no quarter and would give none in the fighting.

These Belgians on the roads were men who had

been temporarily sent back to "recuperate," and while at this work they enjoyed good food, warm quarters, and sleep. At eleven o'clock every morning a very fine motor kitchen would pass along the road. Each man had his canteen ready, the cook ladled out to him a good helping of mashed potatoes, boiled mutton, and thick gravy, and another cook handed him a big chunk of white bread. It was all done very expeditiously and in good order. After getting his share each man would sit on his rolled-up overcoat on the roadside and spoon the mutton and potatoes into his mouth with the bread. Knives and forks and spoons, after all, are really only luxuries.

The roads were in a frightful state during these November weeks. The narrow *pavé* was full of ruts, deep and dangerous, and skirted on either side by a slope of boggy quagmire churned up by the wheels of hundreds of heavy motor transports, and beyond this again on either side was a deep ditch.

Any skidding motor would land in the ditch, and the righting of these embedded cars was at times a titanic task, productive of much loss of temper and bad language.

The narrow *pavé* would not permit of two vehicles crossing abreast, and when two met, neither wished to surrender the "crown of the causeway." It was a point of honour not to budge and to wear down the other side by abusive epithets. Uncle Toby used to say that our army swore horribly in Flanders, but the swearing in Toby's day was not a patch on the rich vocabulary and full-blooded oaths of our London taxi-drivers in Flanders in 1914.

The London taxi-driver, always eloquent, reached his highest flights when addressing the quivering blancmange-like mud of a Belgian road.

I have seen old French non-commissioned officers who probably did not know a single word of what was said on these occasions, but who envisaged the situation perfectly, stand by with approving and admiring faces while the driver was embracing in his comprehensive abuse all things living and dead, the heavens above, the earth beneath, and the waters under the earth.

At Ouderdom we met Alphonse, soldier of France. Two medical officers were one morning sipping some red wine in an *estaminet* in the village when in swaggered a very small French soldier.

He had a boy's face and figure and voice, but bore the assured manner of a man of the world. He was small even for a French boy. A carbine was swung across his back, and his belt carried a bayonet and cartridges. He wore the French blue overcoat with the ends tucked up in the approved style and with the buttons polished and bright. His little legs were encased in the familiar red trousers tucked into heavy boots several sizes too large for him, and his *képi* was placed on his small, closely cropped head at a jaunty angle. Such was Alphonse, the complete soldier of France, full private in a famous Parisian rifle battalion.

Alphonse swaggered into the café, ordered his glass of red wine with the *sang-froid* and assurance of a veteran grenadier, and tossed it off as easily as a Falstaff.

"How old are you, Alphonse?" "But fourteen years, mon officier." "Have you killed many Germans?" "But yes, perhaps thirteen, perhaps fifteen; who can tell when one is fighting every day? But certainly I kill many Bosches." "And with what did you kill them, Alphonse?" "Avec mon carabine"—this with a smack of his hand on the barrel of the gun. A smart soldierly salute, and our gallant killer of thirteen, perhaps fifteen, peaceful, amiable German soldiers strode out of the café.

A corporal of Alphonse's regiment told us that at the beginning of the war Alphonse was a young devil of a gamin in Paris. In his leisure moments he sold newspapers in the streets, and in his working hours he was up to some devilry.

When this regiment marched out of Paris towards the frontier Alphonse marched alongside it, a bright-eyed, hopeful, cheerful youth clad in ragged clothes and down-at-heel boots. He was told to go home, but said that he had no home and was going instead to kill Germans. So in the good French way the regiment adopted Alphonse, gave him a uniform and a gun, and a new pair of boots, and took him on the strength.

The little gamin turned out a very cunning soldier. He was a dead shot, and the corporal assured us that he had accounted for a good many of the enemy. At night Alphonse would crawl out of the trenches and scout well into the enemy lines. Frequently he brought back valuable information of preparations for a German surprise attack. He was so small and so cute that he escaped observation.

In December Alphonse was presented to President Poincaré on one of his many visits to the French front, and the President promised him a commission and the Legion d'Honneur when he should reach the age of twenty-one years. I have grave fears for the gallant, snub-nosed, blue-eyed Alphonse, young in years but old in sin. He is already too fond of the rich red wine of France, and scouting at night inside the enemy lines is a duty full of peril. But Alphonse can teach a lesson in patriotism that many a flower-socked, straw-hatted knut on a London promenade would do well to learn.

The Flemings are very devout Catholics, perhaps the most Catholic of all peoples to-day; so our ambulance was given the hall-mark of respectability because we had with it a Monsignor, The presence of a Catholic prelate with our ambulance, distinguished it in a notable degree from all other ambulances, and we tried to live up to our presumed reputation.

Whenever Monsignor appeared on the roads near Ouderdom the Belgian soldiers would immediately stop work and, carrying their pickaxes and shovels, crowd round him for a talk and the latest news. Monsignor was a good linguist and a cheerful optimist, and never handed on any bad news to the soldiers. One morning he was asked for news, and appealed to me what to say. We told them that the Russians had another victory, and that the German dead could be counted by thousands. This was very palatable and thoroughly appreciated. We were not asked to give any details of the victory, which was perhaps fortunate.

Monsignor would sometimes walk along this road with his hands behind his back and with two or three cigarettes sticking out prominently from between his fingers. The Belgian soldiers would then stalk after him, with broad grins on their faces, and pull away a cigarette. Monsignor never looked behind. That would not be playing the game at all, but his eyes would twinkle, and I have no doubt whatever that he hugely enjoyed the fun.

There were days when Monsignor had a wardrobe consisting of but one shirt and one pair of trousers—the other articles of apparel had all been given away. Then he would begin again to collect mufflers and socks when supplies came in, and hand them out almost immediately to some poor devils who had nothing. If our chaplain appeared any day to be more cheerful than usual, one could make quite sure that he had just given away his boots or his shirt or his towel to some poor French, Belgian, or British Tommy. The only thing he kept a tight hold on was his toothbrush.

One day Monsignor appeared with a cardboard box in his hand and told us that he was going to Renninghelst, a small town about two miles from our headquarters. Lieutenant X—— and myself asked leave to accompany him. We had to ask permission, for Monsignor was a senior chaplain and a lieutenant-colonel in rank, although he never said anything about that. We discovered it accidentally. Being a colonel interested him only in a vague impersonal sort of way. He told us once that a soldier is diffident and shy before a colonel, but is natural and communicative to his minister or priest who is not flagged and starred.

On this lovely winter morning, when the whole countryside was white with frozen snow, we had a sharp bracing walk to the curious old town, then the headquarters of General B—— and his staff of a French Division. The village streets were packed full of French and Belgian soldiery, from Spahis to Alpine Chasseurs. We worked our way round the carts and through the jostling men to a little shop opposite the church. Monsignor was hailed joyfully by many of his old friends, who on this particular morning were not working on the roads.

The mystery of the cardboard box was then unravelled, for after cutting the string and throwing away the cover we saw that it was full of small religious medals and scapularies. There was a big rush for the medals, and we were all squeezed up together by the pressing soldiers, hundreds of whom were holding their grimy paws out for the metal discs. As Monsignor was hard at work I took a hand also and helped in the distribution. At last all were gone. Hundreds more men had come up with hands out, but had to leave unsatisfied. I asked Monsignor if the medals lost any virtue by having been handed out by me, a Protestant. He assured me that it was all right, as the Belgians and French must have thought I was a good Catholic.

Every Field Ambulance has two chaplains attached to it. Ours had a Church of England one and a Roman Catholic. Another ambulance would have perhaps a Wesleyan and a Catholic, or a Presbyterian and an Anglican. These chaplains were not designed for the spiritual needs of the ambulance men, but as each ambulance kept in touch with a brigade consisting of four battalions, the chaplain could also, by being with the ambulance headquarters, keep in touch with the brigade, and could also meet the wounded brought in from that brigade, administer the rites of the Church to those requiring it, and bury the dead. The chaplains did not restrict themselves to the men of their own faith, but helped and worked all they knew for all. After all, an ambulance station full of wounded men is not the place for religious exercises, and a wise chaplain helped in making the men as comfortable as possible, bringing round soup, taking off boots, distributing cigarettes and tobacco, writing letters and "gossiping"—the wounded like some one to talk to them and to talk to, and the chaplains could make a "cheery atmosphere" even in such a gloomy place as a barn full of recently wounded men. Most of the chaplains had a good sense of proportion. Some had not. One bleak, miserable day, I saw a well-meaning but mournful chaplain go up to a lorry full of wounded men packed close together on the straw, uncomfortable and shivering and miserable. He handed to each of them a small religious tract exhorting him to read it. The men took them with a polite "Thank you, sir," but their faces displayed no enthusiasm. This was not the time for tracts. Shortly afterwards another chaplain, a man of the world, came up to the lorry with a "Cheer up, boys. You'll soon be in warm comfortable quarters. Have you any smokes?" The men had none, and out came a dozen packets of Woodbine cigarettes from the chaplain's pockets and two boxes of matches. The expression on the men's faces altered at once. The atmosphere had altered, the sense of proportion had been restored.

Men in hospital like to hear good news. I knew one chaplain who managed never to go into a room full of wounded and sick men without bringing some cheery report for everybody. He never actually fabricated news, but he had a wonderful gift of exaggeration. If we were in the same position, we had "held the line against incredible odds." If the French had taken an enemy trench, "they had driven a wedge into the German position and produced consternation." If Russian cavalry had made a reconnaissance in the Masurian Lakes, "they were sweeping like locusts all over East Prussia, and had set fire to the Kaiser's favourite hunting-lodge."

The men never inquired about details, general statements were quite good enough.

This was better than telling men that the "war would be a terribly long one; that we would have to make great sacrifices; but, please God, we would win in the end." I have heard a chaplain talk like this to wounded men, and I knew that he "wasn't delivering the right goods."

Renninghelst is a large village, or rather a very small town. It is situated close to the Franco-Belgian frontier, and at this period was of importance as an ambulance centre for wounded French and Belgians who were occupying the line of trenches in the front. The country all round is real Flanders land—flat, low-lying, damp, and uninviting. The renowned Mont de Cats can be seen from it, and round this *mont* some hard fighting was taking place. The old village has a queer Dutch-looking church with a closely packed graveyard around it, planted thickly with stone and iron crosses to the memory of ancient departed burghers, whose Flemish-Dutch names are inscribed there to commemorate their ages and their virtues. Eighty, eighty-five, and ninety seemed to be the usual age of these old burghers for slipping off this mortal coil in this quiet sleepy old place in Southern Belgium. There are many new graves now round the Renninghelst countryside, and they are for men who have died young, suddenly, and in the springtime of their days. The interior of this old Flemish church is lofty, and has little in the way of adornment, for there are no millionaires in its congregation to give great stained-glass windows or carved pulpits.

On my first visit to the church it was full of French soldiers, some sleeping and others lolling round on the straw that thickly covered the stone floor. A big group were crowded round a charcoal brazier warming themselves and watching the progress of a savoury stew. The French soldiers are wonderful cooks, and the stew this day was to be a good one, for the *pièce de résistance* was a fine fat hare which had been caught that morning near the front. The two cooks were exercising great care to make the stew a success, and the air of the place was a cheerful, expectant one.

Some days after this visit I was again at Renninghelst, and the church was now a temporary hospital. The floor was still covered with straw, but wounded men were lying close together on it. The charcoal brazier was still there and giving out a welcome heat on this cold wintry day. Ambulance waggons were in the street next the church full of wounded soldiers, and more were coming up the road.

French army surgeons were busy amongst the red-breeched men in the church, and three of them were engaged round an improvised operating table near the altar, where a man deeply under chloroform was having his jaw wired with silver wire for a bad fracture from a piece of shell.

The old white-haired, weary-looking priest of the parish was leaning over a dying man and bending his head low to catch the last faint whispers. Some women of the village were carrying round cups of hot broth to the men propped along the wall, and others were hurrying in with blankets and pillows.

One soldier I observed to be very blanched and tossing restlessly on his straw. Restlessness is always an important sign in wounded men, and on going up to this poor devil and turning down his rough blanket the cause of the trouble was apparent. He was bleeding freely through a bandaged wound of the leg. The dressings were soaked with blood, and as the French surgeons were occupied I broke a professional rule and treated this patient without asking his doctor's permission. The bleeding was soon controlled, and the threatened death from hæmorrhage averted.

As I was completing the last turns of the bandage a voice murmured over my shoulder, "Vive l'entente cordiale." The speaker was the chief surgeon, just released from his work on the operating table. He thanked me for helping, and said that he and his two assistants had been up all night, and had been very busy. Most of the men had been wounded by shrapnel. Shrapnel makes very bad wounds; it rips, tears, and lacerates the tissues, and repair is often impossible in face of the anatomical devastation. The French were having a great deal of trouble with their wounds, as we were also. All the wounds became septic. There is very little clean surgery in this war. The wounds rarely heal by first intention, and a fractured, splintered bone meant months of rest and painful dressings in hospital and a tardy convalescence.

The fighting all along this front had been extraordinarily severe. The French hospitals and the French medical staff were taxed to the utmost. Every available fighting man was in the trenches or waiting as supports. The German hammer was making mighty swings on the Allied anvil, and nowhere were the blows so heavy and so long sustained as on that famous Ypres salient. It was bent and dented, but not broken. The character of the fighting can be grasped from two incidents. One famous infantry regiment left England at full strength. All of its original officers were killed, wounded, or missing. Of the second lot of officers, all were killed, wounded, or missing. Its third supply of officers were now grimly up against the same chain of events.

One of the first British Divisions left England with 12,000 men and 400 officers. When it was withdrawn from the front to rest and refit, it could only muster 2336 men and 44 officers !

A famous French regiment with a long roll of battle honours went into action one frosty morning near Reims. It went forward a gleaming column of more than a thousand bayonets. Two days afterwards forty-nine men, led by an old bearded sergeant, marched back. These were all that were left. The sergeant had a bloody bandage across his forehead—he had lost an eye—but the French Brigadier-General embraced and kissed him on the cheek. The French officers standing near stood rigidly at the salute, and tears were running down their cheeks.

The losses on our side were heavy indeed, but on the German side I am glad to know that they were colossal. The annihilation of German battalions and brigades is an argument that the Germans fully understand, and the only thing that will convince the German that the game is up is heavy and continuous loss of fighting men and difficulty in filling their ranks. This sounds very brutal, but we are living in a hard age.

I was much struck by the splendid way the women of this small Belgian town rallied round to help the wounded. We found the same thing in France; no trouble was too great, and all was done so cheerfully and sympathetically. This is the "women's day" in France. One cannot help admiring their courage and ability in France's hour of trial. Husbands, sons, brothers, fathers—all are on the frontier, and the women carry on the business of France. They make the most stupendous sacrifices and exhibit a sublime patience. None are so joyful as the women when a French victory is announced, and none so pitiful as they when the wounded, the corollary to every victory, arrive at the towns and villages.

This war, which the German has carried on with an animal ferocity and a degenerate lust unequalled in history, has demonstrated to the world the unfaltering nobility of character of the French woman, and that her fervent soul can rise serene and cool in the midst of the most appalling troubles.

When our troops landed at Le Havre in August, it was noticed at once what a big part the women were taking in the business life of the place. There were women conductors on the trams, women in the tobacconist shops, women in the cafés as attendants, in the streets selling newspapers, and in all the big *magasins*.

In Rouen, women conducted coal and timber yards, vegetable and produce businesses, bakeries, butcheries, fishmongeries, grocers' and ironmongers' stores. Women drove carts and waggons, acted as tally clerks on wharves, did everything, in fact—and did it all soberly, quietly, and well. They were always tidy, smart, and cheerful, and did not stop work at eleven o'clock for a glass of beer, or spend many quarters of hours filling and lighting pipes of tobacco.

One woman I know—a rosy-cheeked, blue-eyed Norman dame—did the catering for a large officers' mess in one of the camps at Rouen. At 5 a.m. she was at the mess tent with her pony-cart laden with wine, vegetables, preserves, and fruit. I have passed her shop at nine o'clock at night and have seen her then busily selling dried fish, pickles, and vinegar to her customers. She told me that she was too busy to sleep. This was in 1915, and she had been running the business with no other help than that of two small daughters since July 1914.

Her husband was on the Argonne front, and she was keeping the flag flying till his return. Incidentally, she was making money. Catering for an officers' mess is fairly lucrative.

On the march from the Marne to the Aisne, and on the Aisne itself, women were to be seen doing ordinary farm work—building stacks, carting in the wheat, driving waggon-loads of hay and peas, milking the cows, making cider and butter, tilling the soil,—and tending the children into the bargain.

The most amazing thing of all was to see women working in the fields behind our batteries only a mile away.

At Venizel, on the Aisne bank, our Engineers were throwing a pontoon bridge across the river under a heavy shrapnel fire. Shells were bursting up and down the river's bank and on the waters of the river, yet about a quarter of a mile behind three women were busily engaged cutting turnips for the cows.

On the march from the Aisne to La Bassée, our Field Ambulance bivouacked at the Château of Longpont. The Comte and Comtesse de M—— were in residence at the château, and we were told by the Comtesse that General von Kluck, commanding the right wing of the invading army, had in August stopped for a day and a night at the château with his *état-major*. We asked how Von Kluck had behaved, and the Comtesse said that he had been *très agréable*. When he arrived, she interviewed him and begged him to respect the old château and its old abbey, the pictures and the tapestries. The General promised that he would do so, and that he would give orders that the villagers in the hamlet near the château gates were not to be molested. It was the apple season, and the apple trees of Longpont were laden with delicious fruit. Von Kluck "asked permission" of the Comtesse for his soldiers to take some apples off the trees. This the Comtesse graciously permitted, and the dusty German soldiery helped themselves to the apples and did not break a branch off a single tree.

The Comtesse provided new eggs and butter and bread for the General's breakfast, and he invited her to honour the meal with her presence. But the Comtesse sent a note that she would not break bread with her country's enemy. This was one of the few châteaux and one of the few villages that the German Saligoth did not destroy or outrage before leaving.

Some German Generals approved of outrages and atrocities, to wit, Rupprecht of Bavaria. Some disapproved, and Von Kluck, it is said, was one of these—but I "hac ma doots."

This leads to one of the blackest pictures of this war—a picture grim and loathsome. It is a subject which the women of France will discuss freely and openly and with a concentrated bitterness that one can readily understand. I have spoken to many educated French women on this subject, and have heard many curious and amazing tales and incidents. The subject is that of the women who have been ravished and outraged by the German soldiery.

Many of these victims, married women and young girls, are to-day pregnant to German fathers, and the burning question with the women of France is how best to help their unfortunate sisters, and what is to be done for the offspring.

In the French Chamber of Deputies the subject has been debated with equal freedom and openness. Leading French newspapers too, such as the *Figaro*, *Le Temps*, *Echo de Paris*, and others, have envisaged the position in powerful and appealing articles.

One journal advocated that in the exceptional circumstances it was perfectly justifiable to carry out abortion and interrupt the period of gestation. Opinions were sought from leading French physicians and from the Academy of Medicine. These unhesitatingly condemned such a course, pointing out that the mission of the medical profession was to save life; and also that the induction of premature labour was at all times a dangerous and risky operation to the mother, and in certain circumstances would be fatal.

The Catholic Church in France spoke strongly and certainly in the same direction, and condemned as utterly wrong and sinful any measure that had for its object the death of the unborn child.

The women of France, however, do not share these latter views.

Arrangements have now been completed for the reception of these pitiful expectant mothers into certain maternity homes, where they will be attended by skilled doctors and nurses at the State expense. After birth the child is to be brought up by the State at some place undeclared. The mother will not see the child at any time, and will know nothing of its future.

The clergy all over Northern France are attending to this matter, and everything will be done as secretly as possible in the unusual circumstances.

No wonder that the French woman speaks of the German soldier as a loathly thing.

CHAPTER XIX.

WE LEAVE BELGIUM.

At the end of November our ambulance was ordered to St. Jans Capelle. We were not sorry to leave our house, with its evil pond and manure heap, and the voice of Madame.

Madame, by the way, was very amiable when we told her that we were to leave. She did not say that she was sorry, but she no longer screeched at our cooks or railed at our men for eating her straw. Just as our ambulance was about to move off, and Madame stood at the door with the first approach to a frosty smile that we had ever seen on her face, a French sergeant and ten men of a balloon section arrived. The sergeant had a lump of chalk in his hand and scrawled on the door, "Ballon. 3 sous Officiers. Hommes x." He brusquely informed Madame that the quarters just vacated by us were to be at once taken by his balloon section. Madame raged and raved, but the sergeant was imperturbable, and suddenly quietened Madame by saying that if she objected very much he would begin to think that she was a German spy. The sergeant told us that as a matter of fact they were not satisfied about Madame's husband's patriotism. We knew that

Madame and her sulky husband would now have a much worse time than when we occupied the house, for at least we tried to give little trouble, and lavishly paid for any vegetables, milk, or food that we got from the farmer. The French insist on the "articles of war," and when they occupy a house they really do occupy it and make themselves very much at home.

This mention of Madame's husband being of doubtful honesty, reminded us of a curious incident that occurred early in our stay at this place. There was another farm close to the one we occupied, and this farm was owned by a man who, we were told, was a cousin of "Monsieur our farmer." At this house a man was stopping who said that he was a refugee from Ypres. He told us that he was a baker from Boston, United States of America, and that he and his wife, who were Belgians, had been visiting their native country when war broke out. He said that his wife and two children were in Brussels when the Germans occupied the city, and that he himself was stopping with a friend in Ypres when the Germans first bombarded it; he then left Ypres and came to stop at this farmer's house. This man used to walk every day along a road which passed behind some French batteries of 75 mm., but one day he did not come back. We asked his farmer friend what had become of him, and he said that he had left to go to America. We thought the circumstance odd at the time, and when our sergeant told us about Madame's husband being under suspicion we asked him if he knew anything about this other man, the

Boston baker. He said that he did, for he had seen the fellow arrested and sent back to be tried for spying. That perhaps explained why Madame did not like us, and why her vituperation and objections were suddenly silenced when the French balloon sergeant talked about German spies.

After leaving the inhospitable cottage-headquarters, our ambulance had a long day's trek over the Belgian frontier to St. Jans Capelle. This place was close to Bailleul. We put our men into billets near at hand and got quarters for ourselves in the Convent, where the sisters gave us a big dormitory full of clean white beds with blankets and sheets. This was indeed luxury after all our roughing times from the Marne till now. We were always perfectly willing to undergo inconvenience and hardships, but none of us ever missed an opportunity of availing himself of the luxuries and amenities of civilisation whenever they presented themselves. We had the fine front room of the Convent for a dining- and sitting-room, and, greatest boon of all, a fire to sit round. The cold was intense at this time, and the whole country was frozen hard in snow and ice. This was the period when frostbite was so terrible to our men in the trenches, and the Clearing Hospitals and Ambulance Stations were so busy treating the frozen men.

It was found necessary to relieve frequently the freezing soldiers in the advanced trenches, and every three days they were allowed out from the terrible mud ditches, with death on the parapet and frostbite at the bottom.

Braziers of burning charcoal were put into the trenches, but were found to be ineffective and harmful to the feet. The people of England did magnificent work in sending out gum boots, skin overcoats, and protectives of all sort, but in spite of all that was done the frostbite incapacitated many men. The recoveries were always slow, and could not be effected at the front, so all these limping men were sent back to England for rest and change. Many methods of treatment were tried for the frostbite, but time alone seemed to be the chief curative factor. In some cases the feet were swollen, and small bloody exudates could be seen under the big toe and the outer side of the foot where the boot pressed. Sometimes the skin was broken and ulcers formed at the site. In other cases toes became completely gangrenous or dead. The feet were rubbed and massaged with various oils and swathed in cotton wool, but wrapping in wool aggravated the suffering, and the men felt much more relief when the feet were left exposed. The worst time for the cold-feet men was from one o'clock to three in the morning. They would often go off to sleep peacefully, but would wake up at these hours suffering excruciating pain in their feet and calves and up the spine. Nothing would relieve this pain but hypodermic injections of morphia. One officer described his state to me, and said that he had been standing in a trench in mud over his boot-tops. At first his feet felt very cold, and he tried to warm them by stamping, but this method of exercise was too sloppy. Then sensation seemed to go and he felt quite comfortable, because although his feet felt very heavy they did not feel cold, only dead. On the fifth day he could hardly walk and had to be helped out of the trenches. He was unable to walk to the ambulance, a short way back, and the feet were found to be so swollen in hospital that the boots had to be cut off. Then the worst time of all came on, for as the circulation gradually returned he suffered diabolical pain in his feet and calves, and this pain was always worst in the early mornings. Eight weeks after having been lifted out of the trench he was still limping about with two sticks, and was making a normal but very slow recovery.

This officer told me that one night the men in his trenches were ordered out to make a bayonet attack, but half of them were in such a condition that they could not crawl out of the trench. Fortunately the Germans were pushed back by those who could, otherwise the poor devils left behind would have been captured or killed.

The Indians round the Bethune district suffered very severely from the frostbite, and these poor men deserved our greatest sympathy during this period, trying and terrible enough to men reared in a fairly rigorous climate like that of England or Scotland. The misery of the life to men who had never lived out of tropical India was enough to wear down any but the stoutest hearts. History will give due credit and praise to these Indians, that they rose superior to their environment and soon proved what sterling good soldiers they are. I visited at an Indian Clearing Hospital the first lot of casualties from the M—— Division. This Clearing Hospital took over the École Jules Ferry at Bethune, and occupied it for a few weeks after our Clearing Hospital had vacated it. The doctors belonged to the Indian Medical Service, and the native Indian doctors belonging to the subordinate medical service acted under the white doctors. Some temporary lieutenants of the Royal Army Medical Corps were also on the staff.

The dusky warriors were arriving in scores, brought in on motor ambulances, and very woeful they looked, covered with mud and bloody bandages. They had not been long at the front, and their first experience of modern war was a very desperate ordeal.

The night was dark and gloomy and a heavy rain was soaking the countryside. The mud-splashed cars dashed into the dripping courtyard, fitfully lit up by the sombre gleams of smoky lanterns tied to posts. Round about were the dark-faced bearers ready to help out the wounded. Those who could walk got out of the ambulances themselves and the stretcher cases were taken out by the bearers. The scene on this night impressed one with the far-reaching character of this war, for here were men from the central plains of India, the far-off frontiers and the slopes of the Himalayas, gathered together in a muddy, marshy region of France, and wounded in trying to hold a line of ditches against the most determined and scientific fighting men of Europe.

> "Rulers alike and subject, splendid the roll-call rings,
> Rajahs and Maharajahs, Kings and the sons of Kings,
> From the land where the skies are molten
> And the suns strike down and parch.
> Out of the East they are marching,
> Into the West they march."

One swarthy Sikh with a fine beard was asked what he thought of the war.

"Sahib, it is a very good war. It is a man's war. The old men, the women, and the children are in the villages. The warriors are out fighting. It is very good." This optimist had got through with a slight wound of the right hand, and perhaps that accounted for his cheery outlook. Most of the wounded on that night looked as if they would have been better pleased to be with "the old men, the women, and the children in the villages."

There is no doubt that the Indians are pleased to be fighting alongside us in this "good war," but they have a respect for the German because he is a fierce fighter, and perhaps also because of his ruthlessness, an attitude which appeals to the Oriental mind.

The Gurkha is a funny little man and a swashbuckler. His small sturdy frame, his slanting, watchful eyes with the glint of the devil in them, his bandolier, rifle, and deadly kukri, with its broad razor-edged blade, make up a picture of force and fighting cunning.

Plaster this man with thick mud, put a bloody bandage round his head, and place him in a dimly lit corner of a dripping court on a dark, rainy night, then indeed he looks a breathing symbol of murder and imminent destruction. When the Gurkha is out "on the job" at night, prowling far from his trenches and within the enemy lines, with no weapon but his broad, sharp knife and with a mind intent on slaying, he is a formidable and fearsome adversary.

At first our Indian troops found it difficult to accustom themselves to the novel form of war in wet, cold trenches, a bad climate, and with every surrounding strange and inhospitable. The loss of their British officers and native non-commissioned officers was at first very heavy, and this discouraged the men, who look so much to their officers who know their language and understand them. But these brave fellows soon "found themselves," and have since those dark October days proved again and again that when the call comes they can be relied upon to fight with as much determination as ever they have done in the past. An experienced British officer of a native regiment told me that what the Indians missed very much in France was opium. He said that the Indian had always been accustomed to his opium in India, that he did not take much, but really was the better for a little. He took it in small quantity as a soporific stimulant, just as our grandfathers took snuff, and he assured me that when the Indians had to meet the hellish conditions of modern war at the front last winter a little opium to each man would have meant a great deal. In this I cordially agree with him, for the medicinal and stimulant effects of small doses of opium are undoubted.

The question of feeding our Indian soldiers was a

difficult one, and required very careful handling. An old Sikh was wounded near Bethune and was taken to the British Clearing Hospital. He refused to take anything but biscuits and water. Fortunately we were able to remove the old ritualist to the native Clearing Hospital, otherwise we would have been at an *impasse.*

Amongst both Hindoos and Mohammedans the caste prejudices and ritualistic ceremonies must be remembered and observed in the providing and killing of animals for consumption. The French also have native troops with them and have the same difficulties to overcome, and this helps us considerably in arranging a joint commissariat scheme. A Sikh soldier will not eat a sheep killed in the Mohammedan method by cutting its throat, and the Mohammedan soldier will not eat a sheep killed in the Sikh method by a slashing stroke on the back of the neck. So there you are. These things do not seem to be very important, but they are important all the same. Ask the Jew who refuses the unclean pork, and the good Churchman who refuses meat on Fridays.

The following story, which I heard at the front, illustrates the accommodating nature of the Gurkha. When his regiments were embarking on the transports at an Indian port, the point arose whether he would eat frozen mutton. The British officers agreed to let the matter be solved by the men. So they called up the Subadar, who, after a little wrinkling of the eyebrow, said, "I think, Sahib, the regiment will be willing to eat the iced sheep provided one of them is always present to see the animal frozen to death."

In Rouen there is an encampment for goats for the Indians, and we were told that these goats were good mountain fellows from the Pyrenees. Four Indians, under the charge of an old, venerable, long-bearded native, used to drive them from their encampment to the Indian convalescent dépôt about two miles outside the city.

The goats, in spite of the shouting and rushing about of the drivers, would not keep their ranks and dress by the right in marching through Normandy's capital city. The delight of the French people, who always turned up in crowds to see the goats march past, passed all bounds when one would make a wild dash up a side street, hotly pursued by an irate turbaned Indian. Another source of great joy was to see the goats march slowly along the train line and hold up the train traffic.

The Indians were always of absorbing interest to the French, and crowds of men and women would walk on a fine afternoon from the city to the Indian dépôt camp for convalescents to see our brown-faced fighting men.

On one winter day in Rouen, just after a heavy fall of snow, a company of French soldiers under a non-commissioned officer was marching past the Indian encampment. The Indians lined up the fence alongside the road and bombarded the French with a rapid fire of snowballs. The French looked surprised, and, forgetting discipline but still keeping their ranks, poured a heavy fusillade of snowballs on the men of India. The incident is illustrative of the good feeling that exists between the French and their Indian allies.

The Abbé Bouchon d'Homme of our hospital at Bethune told me with great glee one morning that the Mayor of the town had had a "poser" put to him by the Indians. One of these had just died from wounds, and he had evidently been a fire-worshipper. The dead man's comrades asked the Mayor of Bethune to provide them with timber, as they wished to burn the deceased in the cemetery of the city. The Mayor was staggered at the request, and although he had, so the Abbé said, some curiosity to see the ceremony of fire carried out, he had to "turn down" the proposition. So the man was buried in the usual way.

Good-bye to the Front.

The Army Headquarters, now that our line had been firmly established and locked firmly on our right with the French and on our left with the Belgians and French, decided to allow a short leave, at intervals, and in rotation, to officers and as many men as possible. The leave was specially designed for those who had been through the retreat, the Marne, and the Aisne. New troops were arriving at the front and gradually taking the place of the veterans temporarily retired to recuperate.

The 5th Division had been amongst the hard knocks from the beginning and we got off early.

I left the front by a motor bus, which conveyed a group of seven officers from Bailleul to Boulogne, and from thence we reached England by the ferry steamer.

It felt uncanny to be away from the sound of the guns. Ever since August our lives had been punctuated with incessant gun-fire; we had roused each morning to the sound of heavy artillery, we had gone to sleep with cannonades for a lullaby, and during the long day had listened to the Devil's Orchestra of lyddite, melinite, shrapnel, and rifle fire; and now away from it all we seemed to live in a curiously still and silent world.

London was a very inviting place to return to. The hot bath, the good bed, the morning newspaper at breakfast had never been so much appreciated before. The rough knocking about and the strain had left its effects on the health of many of us, and these four days' rest and recuperation, mental and physical, were a godsend.

At the end of the holiday I was appointed Surgical Specialist to a Base Hospital in Rouen, and for a time my lines were cast in quieter waters. But the allurement of the front — the call of the wild with its excitements and uncertainties — lasted for some time longer. It is a curious fact, but true, that the men at the front would like to get to the Base, and when they get there they want to return to the front. "Those behind say forward, and those in front say back."

The memories of days spent at the front can never

be quite forgotten. Time may blunt the clearness of outline of some of the incidents in a hazy mist, but there are others that will stand out clear and undimmed to the last.

The surgeon sees the very seamy side of war. He comes close to the men stricken down in the field, helpless and bleeding and in pain. He stands by them in their dark hours in hospital and by their bedsides when they die.

While the world is hearing the earthquake voice of Victory, he is perhaps kneeling on the straw easing the path to death of a dying man, one of the victors in the fight, or perhaps operating in a mean cottage, surrounded by wounded men waiting their turn on the table.

The gallant charge, the brave defence, the storming of the enemy's position are heralded in dispatches and in song and story, but translated into the note-book of the "Surgeon in Khaki" they represent many dead, many wounded, much crippling and mutilation, tears, distress, and broken hearts.

I have seen brave men die the death in battle—changed in a second of time from forceful, vital, volcanic energy to still, inanimate rest. I have seen mortally wounded men pass uncomplainingly and composedly to the valley of the shadow, and I have seen faces become anxious and troubled at the thought of those dear and loving ones left behind and of the aching hearts and tears.

I have written letters of farewell from dying men

and officers to wives and sweethearts and children, and have felt the horror and misery of it all. It is a sad and mournful sight to see brave young men die.

Yet, though the life of the "Surgeon in Khaki" is amidst this aftermath of battle, he has the infinite satisfaction of knowing that he can, and does, hold out a hand of help to the hurt and maimed soldier crawling out of the welter of blood and destruction, and that he is doing the work of the Compassionate and Pitying One.

> "Affliction's sons are brothers in distress,
> A brother to relieve! How exquisite the Bliss."

This war has brought out many faults in our national life, but it has also brought out many shining virtues, and to the Faith and Hope of the people in the prowess of the soldiers, we must add the Charity shown by the people of this Empire to our sick and wounded. By subscriptions to ambulance funds, Red Cross funds, and hospitals, and by doing all that was humanly possible to help those hurt in battle, the people of to-day have made a name that posterity will honour and strive in vain to equal. They have also helped the Belgian and Serbian Red Cross movements and have shown that

> "Kindness in another's trouble,
> Courage in your own,"

which is always so admirable a trait.

Our fighting men are magnificent, and the hardihood and patient endurance of our wounded are beyond all praise. I have seen our men in actual fight, I have watched the French gunners at work and seen the French infantry charge with the bayonet and throw back a German rush, and I feel a complete confidence of the ultimate final success of the Allied arms—for to such men is given the Victory.

THE END.